HR INNOVATION-SUPPORT STRATEGY

A Practical Guide for Making Workforce Innovation an Everyday HR Function

DAVID MASUMBA

Printed in the United States of America

Publisher: KDP

ISBN Paperback:

Beloved wife, Mujina and our children Waana and Luwi

TABLE OF CONTENTS

HR leaders Challenged to Enhance Strategic Contribution

Meaning of Strategic HR

HR Missing the Opportunity to Drive Innovation

HR Lacking the Tools and Abilities to Lead Workforce Innovation

HR Innovation-Support Strategy

Factor 1: Understand the Reason for the HR Innovation-Support Strategy

Factor 2: Gain the Confidence of the Organization to Drive Innovation

Factor 3: Build a Case to the CEO and other C-suite Executives

Factor 4: Whether the Organization has Existing Innovation-Related Support Programs

Category A: Innovation Management Programs

Category B: Innovation Engagement Programs

Category C: Innovative Thinking Programs

Step 1: Appointment of HR Committee

Step 2: Preliminary Aspects to Consider

Step 3: Content and Format for the Innovation-Support Strategy
Implementation Plan

Description of the Evaluation Model

Three-step Evaluation Model:

    Step 1: Monitoring the Implementation Plan

    Step 2: Measuring Innovation Performance

    Step 3: Structuring an Evaluation Report

Conclusion and Improvements

PREFACE

"Innovation is driven by people, and HR is missing a golden opportunity in driving innovation in their companies because for the most part, HR practitioners have no program or process to drive workforce innovation. Unfortunately, when the leadership is needed in innovation, HR isn't even a player."

Dr. John Sullivan

"Human capital functions such as HR play a significant role in making innovation systemic, but how often do you hear about their involvement?"

Karen B. Paul, PhD. —Manager, Talent Assessment, 3M

In today's innovation-driven global economy, work performance trends are now shifting away from "routine work" toward innovation performance. Now more than ever, companies across industries are now making innovation everyone's job: From senior leadership to the most junior employee.

This is easier said than done. Creating an environment across the functional units of an organization in which everyone is involved in driving innovation does not happen naturally. Functional units must adopt deliberate leadership roles to lead innovation in a sustainable, results-driven manner.

The question is: how will HR lead workforce innovation?

Since the natural role of HR is to design interventions aimed at unlocking organizational human capital, it should naturally provide the leadership to drive the culture of innovation across functional units.

The challenge for HR is how to continually create and implement innovation-support strategies and programs that contribute to institutionalizing workforce innovation. Certainly, HR professionals cannot contribute to driving the culture of innovation using traditional

HR tools and practices. To begin the process of institutionalizing innovation, you must start with a framework that can garner full participation from all functional units and workforces. This book provides HR with tools to design and implement innovation-support programs aimed at making innovation a habitual practice across functional units.

Chapter 1

INTRODUCTION

"Products don't innovate, people do. This statement underpins the key role HR plays—or should play—in cultivating a consistent and replicable method for driving innovation in organizations."

~ *Center for Advanced Human Resource Studies- Cornell University (USA)*

Overview

In his poem, *The Hunting of the Snark*, Lewis Carroll writes, "If you don't know where you are going, any road will take you there." How does this quote relate to the title and purpose of this book? As you will learn in this chapter, the information focuses on the role of HR in fostering a culture of innovation in organizations and suggests that the HR innovation-support strategy is the path to this goal. It is difficult for HR to make meaningful contribution to workforce innovation without an effective path.

It is important to understand from the onset that creating a culture of innovation across functional units of an organization requires a methodical approach. There must be a design and implementation of a clear path to do it. This book focuses on how HR can lead the culture of innovation through the implementation of the HR innovation-support strategy.

In this Chapter

We focus on three things:

- Providing reasons why an HR innovation-support strategy is a vital tool for HR to drive workforce innovation
- Describing what an HR innovation-support strategy entails
- Structure of the book

The three aspects are reflected in the following sub-topics:

1. HR leaders challenged to assume a more strategic role
2. Meaning of strategic HR
3. HR missing the opportunity to drive innovation
4. HR innovation-support strategy

1. HR leaders Challenged to Enhance Strategic Contribution

There is a widely held view that HR is still perceived as an administrative role whose strategic impact on an organization is difficult to see. It focuses largely on operational functions, such as hiring and firing, benefits, compliance issues, employee grievances, and nothing much in terms of strategic contributions. Some professional reports, industry commentators, and academics have gone so far as to suggest that HR's function is the last bastion of bureaucracy and that HR professionals still serve as the policing arm of the executive management.

Dave Ulrich, renowned HR expert and Professor of Business at the University of Michigan, has long argued that HR leaders should assume more vital and strategic roles, rather than merely keeping busy with everyday stuff like policies, pension, payroll, and picnics.

Ulrich believes that HR leaders should strive to build and strengthen unique strategic capabilities. Similarly, Becker B et al., observes that, in most cases, the CEO and senior line managers are—at best—skeptical of HR's role in contributing to realizing the organization's strategic goals. "As in many firms, executives want to believe that people are their most important asset, but they just cannot understand how the HR function can make that vision a reality", adds Becker B et al. In a survey for about 555 senior executives, including 226 CEOs conducted by the UK's *Economist Intelligence,* they were asked to rate the performance within various areas of their business. Survey respondents slammed their HR functions, with more respondents assessing the performance of their HR units *bad* rather than *good.* "No other function—not even the notoriously unloved IT department—came close to being this unappreciated", the report indicated. Almost a third of the respondents rated HR a 4 or 5 (5 being poor) in terms of strategic contribution.

This continues to be the perception. In an Interview with *Harvard Business Review Publishing*, former Procter & Gamble CEO, A.G. Lafley, was asked how he conducted his innovation performance review meetings at Procter & Gamble. Lafley outlined that as CEO he made sure that he was responsible for all innovation strategy reviews. During the reviews, he made sure all critical players and leaders at Procter & Gamble were present, including Head of Design, Head of Consumer Understanding, Head of R&D, and Head of Business Development. Notice who is not mentioned? HR! Isn't innovation exclusively about unlocking people's imaginative potential? Shouldn't this be a core function of HR? Doesn't this exemplify how HR function is still regarded as a non-strategic function in many organizations? This brings us to *what strategic HR is.*

2.   The Meaning of Strategic HR

Before we get into the details of what strategic HR entails, I am reminded of an interesting instance at one of the UK universities I attended years ago. A graduate student asked a professor how strategic one of the postgraduate HR classes was because according to the student, he had done most of the stuff he was learning in the postgraduate program at the undergraduate level in his country. The professor tried his best to interpret a number of aspects that made up the "strategic context" of the university's HR program. Long story short, I don't remember whether or not the student indicated that he was satisfied with the explanation because his professor didn't know how to answer the question.

A strategic HR approach means taking a long-term, big-picture approach to HR and operating initiatives directly connected to major corporate strategy long-term objectives. Rather than focusing on operational HR issues, a strategic focus would mean addressing and solving business problems and contributing to business results through the effective use of people management programs. Strategic HR focuses on real drivers of value proposition, and not just a bunch of routine administrative and policy activities.

Examples of HR Strategic Roles

- Traceable contributions in various core areas of an organization, such as product development, customer satisfaction, sales growth, and innovation performance
- Participation in a traceable contribution to the achievement of overall profitability and growth goals of the organization

This means that if HR is to be perceived to be contributing to achieving the strategic goals of an organization, HR leaders must be seen to understand and articulate corporate strategy goals of the company. Also, understand the functional strategies of other departments, especially core functional units. Understanding should be expressed by the articulation and alignment of the corporate strategy and functional strategies to HR support strategies and functional activities. One of the purposes of this book is to show how innovation is an effective strategy for building sustainable growth and competitiveness of a company, thus, the need for HR to embrace the role of driving workforce innovation, which to a greater extent enhances the strategic role of HR.

3. HR Missing the Opportunity to Drive Innovation

Work performance trends are now shifting away from routine tasks and more toward innovation performance. We are beginning to see companies across industries making innovation everyone's job. Since the role of HR is to design interventions aimed at unlocking organizational human capital and innovation being a process that involves generating innovative ideas, HR is best suited for driving workforce innovation. HR has their hands on the names and positions of all employees, why wouldn't it start there?

It is now common knowledge that we are in an era of innovation leadership. Gary Hamel, the world-renowned author and business thought leader is often quoted to have said, *"Twenty years ago, the challenge in corporations was quality. Ten years ago, the challenge was re-engineering. Today, the challenge is innovation."*

In today's world of intense competition, innovation is now being perceived as the only effective strategy for sustaining corporate growth, profitability, competitiveness and resilience (in times of an economic downturn). Studies have consistently, observed that highly innovative companies have higher growth and higher profits than less innovative or non-innovative ones. Highly innovative companies tend to be resilient and also easily rebound during economic downturns.

In my ten years of offering innovation training and consulting work in a number of countries, I've interacted with many business executives and professionals across industries and accessed numerous studies and reports on innovation. They all unequivocally state one thing…and that is innovation is the most effective strategy for sustaining business growth and competitiveness; innovation is the leading predictor of future growth and profitability of an organization; and innovation is a driver of institutional quality in public service institutions and national economic development. One of the OECD (Organization for Economic Cooperation and Development) reports elaborated on the importance of innovation driving economic growth and the human development of countries.

"Our understanding of what drives national prosperity has evolved over time. Natural resources, population growth, industrialization, geography, climate and military--------all have played a role in the past. There is a newcomer to the modern engines of economic growth------innovation capabilities of a country". Stated of the reports. Harvard economist, Elhanna Helpman notes in his book, *The Mystery of Economic Growth,* that, recent "new growth" economics research has shown that capital accumulation is not the principal factor driving growth. He cites compelling evidence that innovation is now a major driver of productivity.

Acknowledging the key role that innovation has played in the economic growth and sustainable competitiveness of the U.S., former President Barack Obama regularly articulated and reminded Americans of how critical innovation is and how his administration made innovation the anchor of its economic policies. In his State of the Union address on January 27, 2010, he made innovation one of the main themes of his speech. "The first step to winning the future," he said, "is encouraging American innovation." During this State of the Union Address, President Obama mentioned the words *innovation* or *innovate* about 11 times. Here are a few more examples that show the focus is on innovation:

- A study by Accenture revealed that ninety three percent of surveyed C-suite executives said the long-term success of their organization's strategy depended on their ability to continuously innovate, and 70% placed innovation among their company's top five priorities.

- In a survey by the Conference Board (a U.S institute that conducts surveys on various topics with CEOs across the globe), out of 776 CEO respondents, about ninety percent of the respondents identified innovation as their top critical challenge.

- According to a 2017 PwC survey, more than 60% of the CEOs are rethinking their HR functional roles so that HR can play a leading role in driving innovation. And 77% of the CEOs indicated that they struggle to find innovation skills they need. In the same study CEOs ranked innovation as the number one business priority.

At the time of writing this book I had a phone conversation with Erik Diaby (not a real name), HR Vice President of a manufacturing company in the Bay Area of California. Diaby was of the view that HR professional associations were of no help when it comes to providing training and awareness programs to help HR professionals develop with skills to contribute to innovation. "Look, for instance," he said. "Many studies in the last 10 or so years have constantly revealed that innovation is a very high priority for most CEOs and other C-suite executives. But how many HR professionals are aware of this?" He went on to say, "I'll be attending the annual SHRM conference from June 23-26, 2019 in Las Vegas, but when you look at the pre-conference workshops and the conference presentations, none focus on the role of HR in advancing innovation. And it's the same with many other conferences by HR associations across the globe—you hardly ever hear these guys focus on innovation, yet innovation is the topic that's keeping CEOs and other C-suite executives awake at night. Not only that, innovation is the only strategic competence that assures sustainable business growth and competitiveness. Isn't the indifference toward innovation by HR associations shocking?" he asked.

Bottom line is that HR is best suited for driving workforce innovation; however, HR is said to be missing the opportunity to drive innovation for lack of tools to make it happen.

4. HR Lacks Tools and Abilities to Lead Workforce Innovation

As mentioned earlier, HR professionals aren't doing much to champion innovation in their organizations, yet their roles are best suited for that. The immediate question would be, why is it that HR is unable to lead workforce innovation?

For more than ten years, I've been engaged in workforce innovation training and consulting, and interacting with organizational leaders on the topic of workforce innovation. I've also conducted reviews of many studies and publications related to leading workforce innovation. My experience is that many HR professionals seem to have the desire to lead workforce innovation, but the problem is that they are inhibited by the lack of tools and abilities to do so.

Some studies and HR experts attest to this. For instance, an IBM survey of global HR leaders revealed that there was an agreement among HR leaders that driving innovation is their number one business challenge, however, many of them did not have the ability to drive innovation. Susan Meisinger, a former President and CEO of the Society for Human Resource Management was quoted by an online publication about HR lacking the skills to drive workforce innovation. "The takeaway for me in all this is we all think these things matter (HR's role in contributing to advancing innovation), but most of us are not doing something about it. It is difficult; if it were easy, we'd all be doing it."

It is clear that HR cannot fulfill this role of driving workforce innovation without the necessary tools. You cannot introduce a new concept and change culture with old tools. It's that simple. In terms of driving workforce innovation:

- You cannot identify innovation talent candidates using traditional recruitment techniques.
- You cannot motivate staff to contribute to innovation by subjecting them to conventional performance appraisals and traditional reward policies.
- You cannot use generic job position descriptions and expect workforces to discharge innovation performance roles effectively.

- You cannot institutionalize innovation by using traditional succession planning approaches.
- In short, you cannot lead innovation without innovation-based leadership tools.

Bottom line is that the desire by HR to contribute to driving workforce innovation in organizations is there. However, the problem is that many HR professionals lack the required tools and skills to transform their desire into action to implement innovation-support practices that would help create a culture of innovation noticeable by everyone in the organization.

5. HR Innovation-Support Strategy

If HR professionals lack the tools and skills to drive workforce innovation, what tools would enable them to do so?

Remember, HR seems to have the desire, but they lack the tools to lead workforce innovation. Indeed, desiring is one thing; but translating that desire into action and contributing to creating HR innovation-support practices while building a culture of innovation is another.

To put it differently, making innovation a culture in an organization is not easy. It is an undertaking that involves a lot of moving parts. As Rowan Gibson (a renowned international innovation expert) puts it: "Making innovation a systemic organizational capability is a complex and multi-faceted challenge. It simply cannot be solved with some Band-Aid or silver bullet. Instead, it requires deep and enduring changes to leadership focus, performance metrics, organization charts, management processes, training programs, incentive, and reward structures. Otherwise, a company's efforts to make a culture of innovation happen will be doomed."

What's in the toolkit?

To answer the question asked earlier (at the beginning of this section), this book has suggested a toolkit of innovation-support tools detailing how HR can make the role of driving workforce innovation across functional units a daily functional activity.

Definition of Terms

Innovation: Innovation as a process that involves identifying a problem or need, generating a new idea that has not been seen on the market before, turning the idea into a solution to address the identified need, then converting the solution into monetary value.

Support: In the context of innovation, the phrase "innovation-support" implies promoting and implementing programs and initiatives aimed at creating a climate of innovation across functional units.

Strategy: The term *strategy* is the most used term in organizations, and there are several publications that have been written about what *strategy* is. From a general sense, the online dictionary Merriam Webster defines *strategy* as "a plan of action designed to achieve a goal".

From a business perspective, the term *strategy* is defined differently. For instance, in their book *Exploring Corporate Strategy* (8th Edition), renowned experts on strategy, Gerry Johnson, et al. (2008) defines strategy as "a long-term direction of the organization expressed in broad statements about the types of action required to achieve objectives". The book goes on to say that the term, *strategy* may be expressed or used in many business contexts such as marketing, finance, HR, new products or services, procurement, operations, etc.

Definition of HR Innovation-Support Strategy

We define HR innovation-support strategy as: A step-by-step process expressed or outlined in detailed statements of how various innovation-related tools, approaches and actions can be applied by HR to implement initiatives aimed at advancing workforce innovation across functional units to achieve an innovation-led organization.

You can also define HR innovation-support strategy as written expressions that describe a process that involves the identification and application of the right innovation-related tools and activities across functional units to create an organizational environment in which every employee is encouraged, motivated, and enabled to take part in advancing innovation in the organization. By doing so, you create a culture of innovation where it is everyone's job across all functional units to drive innovation.

The four phases of preparation and implementation of the HR innovation-support strategy are expressed in figure 1-1, below:

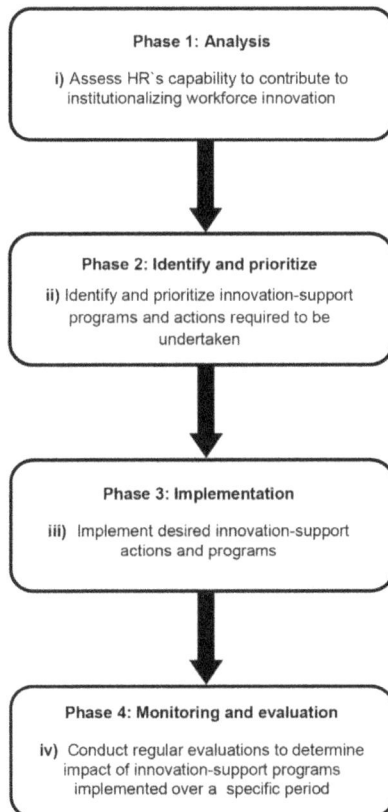

Phase 1: Analysis

i) Assess HR's capability to contribute to institutionalizing workforce innovation

Phase 2: Identify and prioritize

ii) Identify and prioritize innovation-support programs and actions required to be undertaken

Phase 3: Implementation

iii) Implement desired innovation-support actions and programs

Phase 4: Monitoring and evaluation

iv) Conduct regular evaluations to determine impact of innovation-support programs implemented over a specific period

Timeline of Activities

Here is an example of the four phases of activities over a period of eleven months. Table 1-1 is an example summary of how each of the phases, programs, and activities of the HR innovation-support strategy are spread over time.

Table 1-1. Example of the HR innovation-support strategy timeline of activities

HR innovation-support strategy timeline		
February	**March**	**April**
Analysis: assessment of factors driving the need and HR's capability to undertake a company-wide HR innovation-support strategy *Identification and prioritization:* of innovation-support programs and actions required to be undertaken		
May	**June**	**July**
Implementation plan: for prioritized innovation-support actions and programs *Action plans:* implementation of specific tasks and activities adopted from the implementation plan		
August	**September**	**October**
Monitoring: the implementation and management of various innovation-support programs and specific tasks and activities		
November	**December**	
Evaluation: determine impact of HR innovation-support strategy programs and actions implemented		

Interpretation of the Term Workforce Innovation

Employee-driven innovation implies creating an organizational climate aimed at encouraging, motivating and enabling all employees to continually take part in advancing innovation. In other words, it is an environment where employees are motivated and enabled to generate various types and degrees of innovative ideas in the context of the organization's business model, functional activities, and in relation to corporate and functional innovation goals and vision.

Structure of the Book

This book is structured into five chapters:

- Introduction (Chapter 1)
- Analysis (Chapter 2)
- Identification and Prioritization of Innovation-Support Programs (Chapter 3)
- Implementation (Chapter 4)
- Evaluation (Chapter 5)

Chapter 2

PHASE 1: ANALYSIS

Overview

In what context is this analysis? This chapter has prescribed four analysis activities (outlined as factors one, two, three and four) that should be taken into consideration when creating an organization-wide HR innovation-support strategy.

In this chapter

We focus on the four factors:

- Factor 1: Understand the reason for the HR innovation-support strategy
- Factor 2: Gain confidence of the organization to drive innovation
- Factor 3: Build a case to CEO and other C-suite executives
- Factor 4: Whether the organization has existing innovation-related support programs

Details of each as follows:

Factor 1: Understand and Communicate the Reason for the HR Innovation-Support Strategy

First and foremost, it is important for HR to understand the reason for adopting an HR innovation-support strategy. That being said, there are many reasons why an HR innovation-support strategy is required in an organization. Some of the reasons include: (1) helping the organization create a culture of innovation, (2) achievement of corporate and functional innovation goals (3) realizing the organizational vison, and (4) internal and external factors influencing the need for creating a culture of innovation. The head of HR must communicate these reasons as part of the starting point for adopting the HR innovation-support. The four reasons are discussed in detail as follows.

Helps the organization create a culture of innovation

Remember, for many years the conventional approach to innovation in organizations has been that innovation is the responsibility of specific functional units and professionals. However, in recent years, many organizations across the globe are now making innovation everyone's job. In other words, most leaders are seeking to create a culture of innovation in which everyone in the organization is responsible for innovation. However, the culture of innovation does not occur naturally; it occurs only if a climate for innovation is created. Creating a climate for innovation across the organization can be realized if an organization implements innovation-support initiatives on a continual basis.

As stated in Chapter One, traditional management models cannot effectively drive and sustain a culture of innovation. What does this mean to HR? It means that HR cannot drive workforce innovation using traditional HR tools and approaches. For instance, HR cannot identify innovation talent candidates using traditional recruitment techniques, they cannot motivate staff to contribute to innovation by subjecting them to conventional performance appraisals, they cannot use generic job position descriptions and expect workforces to discharge innovation performance duties and responsibilities, and they cannot institutionalize innovation by using traditional succession planning approaches, etc. Since the role of HR is to design interventions aimed at unlocking human capital to generate innovative ideas, HR is best suited for driving workforce innovation by continually implementing HR innovation-oriented tools and practices such as those covered in this book.

Achievement of corporate and functional innovation goals

One of the vital practices for creating a culture of innovation is to regularly set corporate and functional innovation goals. So, one of the purposes of implementing an HR innovation-support strategy is to help the organization achieve corporate and functional unit innovation goals on a continual basis. What are innovation goals? In my book, *Leadership for Innovation,* I defined innovation goals as the following: statements expressing the desired future state of innovation performance to be attained within a specified period in the context of the specified level of the organization (i.e., individual level, departmental level, corporate level). The illustration below in figure 2-1 is a simple innovation-corporate goal-setting flowchart.

Figure 2-1. Innovation-corporate goal-setting flowchart

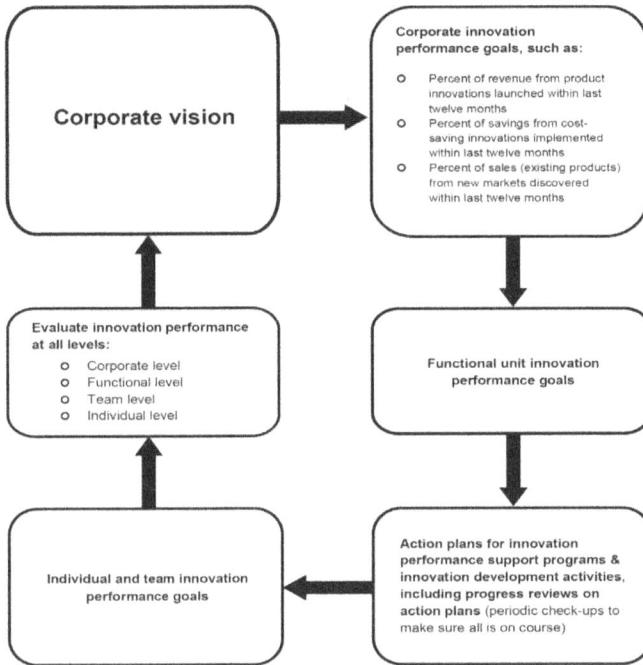

Corporate vision

Corporate innovation performance goals, such as:

- o Percent of revenue from product innovations launched within last twelve months
- o Percent of savings from cost-saving innovations implemented within last twelve months
- o Percent of sales (existing products) from new markets discovered within last twelve months

Evaluate innovation performance at all levels:

- o Corporate level
- o Functional level
- o Team level
- o Individual level

Functional unit innovation performance goals

Individual and team innovation performance goals

Action plans for innovation performance support programs & innovation development activities, including progress reviews on action plans (periodic check-ups to make sure all is on course)

Adapted from Chapter Thirteen
of the *Leadership for Innovation*

Realizing the organizational vision

One of the single most important reasons why many organizations pursue innovation is to realize the organizational vision, and because of this the connection between innovation and realizing the organizational vision is one of the aspects HR leaders could use to inform HR teams in the organization as reason for adopting HR innovation-support strategy.

When formulating the message about the link between workforce innovation and realizing the organizational vision, it is important for HR to distinguish between *organizational vision* and *corporate strategy*. This is because innovation is a form of strategy, and according to a number of publications, many organizational leaders seem to have difficulties in communicating to workforces about how an organizational vision differs from a corporate strategy. That being said, what is an organizational vision? This book defines *organizational vision* as a picture expressed in a statement of what the organization should be like after a specific period. In other words, it's an expression of a vision for the organization's future. On the other hand, a strategy is *what will get the company from where it is now to where it wants to be after the specified period.* In other words, strategy is how a company intends to realize its vision. Stated differently, vision answers the question, *what do we want our organization to be like in the next three to five years?* Strategy answers the question, *how are we going to get there?*

Usually, companies have different perspectives on how to formulate their visions. Some companies have a one-sentence vision statement; whereas others take a multidimensional approach in which the organizational vision is expressed from more than one perspective, such as two, three, or four vision perspectives focusing on core concepts. For example, one company's organizational vision might consist of the following four vision perspectives:

- *Market share:* Takes into account what the company intends to be like in relation to market share within a defined time frame.

- *Market leadership:* Outlines the company's vision to be a market leader in a particular industry over a specified period of time.

- *Revenue vision:* Outlines the financial vision of the company over a specified period. In other words, how much revenue does the company intend to generate in the next three to five years?

- *Shareholder-value vision:* Outlines the desired percentage of growth in dividends over a specified period.

Internal and external factors

As part of the process for educating HR teams about adopting an HR innovation-support strategy, it is important for the HR leadership to inform and educate HR team members about the internal and external factors that have necessitated the company to adopt a culture of innovation. Figure 2-2 outlines some examples of external and internal factors.

Figure 2-2. Examples of external and internal factors

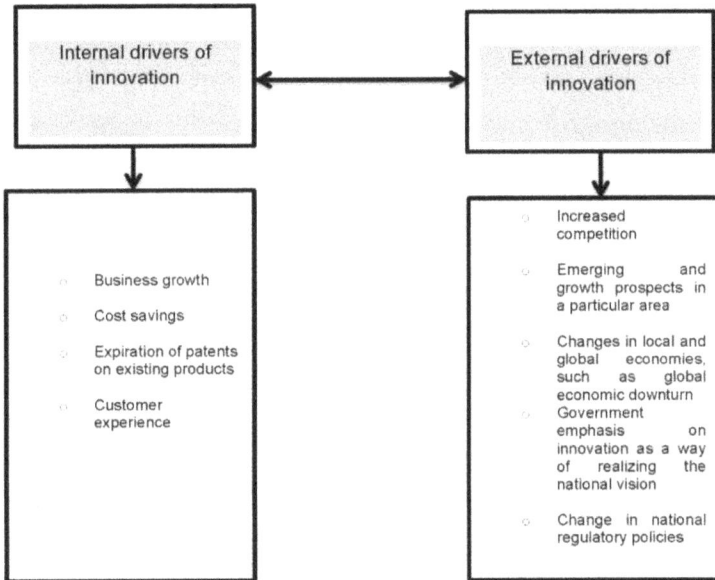

Adapted from Chapter Eight of the *Leadership for Innovation*

As outlined above, there are numerous internal and external factors that influence organizations to implement innovation strategies on an ongoing basis and create a culture of innovation. Chapter Eight (*Educating Workforces about the Drivers of Innovation*) of the *Leadership for Innovation*, describes in detail these examples.

Factor 2: Gain Confidence of the Organization to Drive Innovation

HR leadership must analyse its self-belief and portray the necessary capabilities to win the confidence of the organization to drive innovation.

Remember, as discussed, the inability of the HR professionals to champion innovation in a noticeable way is due to lack of necessary tools and skills to make it happen. Because of this, many organizational leaders tend to have little confidence in HR's ability to play a leading role in creating a culture of innovation. What does this entail in relation to the role of HR in developing and implementing an innovation-support strategy? It means that very few people in the organization will buy into the idea that HR can assume the role of championing and driving innovation across functional units in a way that will produce meaningful monetary results to the organization. As stated in Chapter One, such skepticism is expected because, traditionally, innovation management has never been associated with HR, because generally, people in corporate world are used to hearing innovation management as domain of functional units like R&D, production, engineering, customer service, IT, marketing etc. So, to hear HR talking about championing organization-wide innovation, will not be taken seriously. Against this backdrop, HR has to do two things. First of all, analyse its self-belief in championing workforce innovation. Second of all, gain confidence of the organization that the HR team has the ability to lead workforce innovation in a way that produces meaningful monetary results to the organization.

Gaining confidence of other functional units in the organization to lead workforce innovation does not occur naturally, it has to be earned. There are many ways to do this. One of them is for HR to instil in the hearts and minds of the top leaders and all workforces that HR is not only best suited (by nature of its roles), but has the capacity to drive workforce innovation and deliver meaningful results. Question is, what approaches should be used to gain confidence of the workforces? There are two approaches that can be applied. Namely, *aspirational* and *informative* styles.

Inspirational

This style involves educating workforces across the organization about HR's ability to make workforce innovation systemic and permanent across functional units. HR would do this by regularly articulating and conveying to workforces across the organization (via different types of communication strategies, including messages and visual illustrations) simple catchphrases about how HR is best suited to drive workforce innovation. Here are some examples of simple catchphrases:

- Which organizational functional unit is, by design, exclusively about leveraging human capital to drive growth in organizations? It's HR.

- Innovation is about ideas! Which functional unit has tools for unlocking human capital to generate innovative ideas? HR.

- Which functional unit has potential tools for identifying innovation talent? HR.

- Which functional unit has tools for rewarding staff to encourage them to innovate? HR.

- Which functional unit has tools for developing innovation goals across functional units? HR.

- Which functional unit has tools to create innovation roles? HR

The above catchphrases could be accompanied by visual illustrations.

Informative

This style involves informing workforces on a regular basis about the innovation-support systems that HR will implement, such as innovation strategies, innovation policies, innovation procedures, innovation goals, and innovation plans and that the organization intends to implement or has implemented strategies to advance innovation across the organization. HR would also communicate its intentions to collaborate with functional units to develop frameworks to measure and report innovation performance of various functional units or divisions of the organization and the whole organization.

Factor 3: Build a Case to CEO and other C-Suite Executives

No matter how passionate or committed the head of HR may be in having HR take a leading role in championing innovation, support of the CEO is obligatory. What does this mean? It entails that the success of HR in driving innovation across functional units of the organization largely depends on the level of support that the CEO dedicates to the innovation cause. Specifically, the HR department must have the support of the CEO in order to drive workforce innovation. This is so because once the CEO gives unwavering support, other C-suite executives will follow suit. The opposite would be the case if the CEO does not support.

Intending to succeed in leading workforce innovation without CEO's support is analogous to planting corn seed in dry sand hoping that the seed will germinate and grow into a plant. It cannot grow because there is no water, and also the soil lacks other essential ingredients necessary for the corn seed to germinate and grow into a plant. Similarly, the CEO provides the "water" (i.e. the support) for HR to succeed in legitimizing itself as the best suited functional unit to drive innovation across the organization.

The head of HR should elucidate value in terms of: (1) Why HR is best suited, and (2) How HR will fulfil the role of championing innovation from which the organization will make meaningful monetary gain. This can be done by communicating clearly to the CEO and other executives about the value proposition of HR involvement in driving workforce innovation. How? For instance, during informal briefings and formal meetings with the CEO and other executives, the head of HR should persuasively communicate, among other things, the following:

- Innovation-support systems that HR will implement—such as innovation strategies, innovation policies, innovation procedures, innovation goals, and innovation plans—that the organization intends to implement or has implemented to advance innovation across the organization.

- Intentions to collaborate with functional units to develop frameworks to measure and report innovation of various functional units or divisions of the organization and the entire organization.

- Career development benefits that will be derived from building workforce innovation abilities by teams across the organization.

- Talent stability and competitive benefits that will be derived from building workforce innovation abilities across the organization.

- State in simple and clear terms why workforce innovation is crucial in relation to the internal and external factors.

Factor 4: Whether the Organization has Existing Innovation-Related Support Programs

The last analysis factor is to determine whether the organization has any existing innovation-related support programs which were implemented in the past. If yes, an outline of such programs must be created. Once created the programs must be integrated accordingly in the three categories of the innovation-support programs of the HR innovation-support strategy under development. Chapters Three and Four discuss in detail the categories of the HR innovation-support programs adopted for this book.

Action plan

The four factors of analysis covered in this chapter will not contribute anything to the process of developing and implementing the HR innovation-support strategy without a simple plan of relevant activities that will need to be conducted to implement and operationalize the four factors considered under analysis. Table 2-1 is an example of a simple action plan template outlining activities aimed at operationalizing the analysis factors identified as part of Phase One of developing and implementing the HR innovation-support strategy.

Table 2-1. Action plan for analysis activities

Objective: *To co-ordinate and implement analysis activities*				
What: Activity to be conducted	**Who:** Name of a person or team to perform the activity	**When:** Timeframe for conducting each activity	**Resources:** Needed to conduct each activity	**Output:** Expected outcome from each of the earmarked activities

Factor 1: Understand and communicate the reason for the HR innovation-support strategy				
Factor 2: Gain confidence of the organization to drive innovation				
Factor 3: Build a case to CEO and other C-suite executives				
Factor 4: Whether the organization has existing innovation-related support programs				

Identify the dates for conducting evaluations to determine how the implementation plan is progressing

Date:	Date:	Date:	Date:	Date:
Outline aspects that you will be evaluated on this date	Outline aspects that you will be evaluated on this date	Outline aspects that you will be evaluated on this date	Outline aspects that you will be evaluated on this date	Outline aspects that you will be evaluated on this date

Chapter 3

PHASE 2: IDENTIFICATION AND PRIORITIZATION OF INNOVATION-SUPPORT PROGRAMS

Overview

In Chapter One we defined HR innovation-support strategy as statements detailing the type of HR innovation-support programs, activities and actions that should be undertaken over a specified period of time to create a culture of innovation in the organization. Also observed in Chapter One, that although HR has the desire to contribute to creating a culture of innovation, the problem is the lack of tools and skills for HR to translate their desire into efforts and knowhow to implement innovation-support practices that would help create a culture of innovation across functional units of the organization.

The question is, what kind of programs, tools, and activities should be identified for inclusion in the HR innovation-support strategy?

In this chapter

We focus on the three categories of innovation-support programs that are essential and have been identified for developing and implementing an HR innovation-support strategy. These are:

- Category A: Innovation Management Programs
- Category B: Innovative Thinking Programs
- Category C: Innovation Engagement Programs

The chapter is separated into two parts. *Part I: Identification of Innovation-Support Programs* and *Part II: Prioritization of Innovation-Support Programs.*

Part I: Identification of Innovation-Support Programs

Part I discusses two things: (1) Three categories of the innovation-support programs (2) what each of the three categories comprise of, and (3) how to apply the tools contained in each category to drive the HR innovation-support strategy.

Category A: Innovation Management Programs

What are innovation management programs or initiatives? Generally, organizations operate through a structure of systems designed specifically to deliver the mission of an organization and, ultimately, realize the company's vision. In terms of creating a culture of innovation, remember that you cannot create a culture of innovation across the organization using traditional, non-innovation-oriented management tools.

This means that if innovation is to be a permanent and ongoing habitual process across functional units of an organization, it is vital for HR to implement organization-wide innovation-support systems. So, the purpose of an HR innovation-support strategy is to help functional units apply various innovation-related tools to make innovation systematic. Systematizing innovation means helping functional units across the organization to adopt innovation-support strategies, policies and procedures, structures, and technologies to contribute to creating and sustaining a culture of innovation across all functional units of the organization.

Examples of Innovation Management Programs

In this section we give examples of innovation management programs that would be adopted for the HR innovation-support strategy. To illustrate, let's assume we are identifying innovation management programs for implementation across the functional units of a fictitious company, Walu Technologies, based in San Francisco, California. The company has the following product categories: software, cloud storage, and cybersecurity. The company has core and support functional units as follows:

Core units

- Product development division, comprising the following units:
  - Software segment
  - Cloud storage segment
  - Cybersecurity segment

- Marketing department, comprising the following units:
  - Product pricing
  - Product delivery process
  - Product promotion
  - New markets
  - Customer service department

- Support units
  - Procurement department
  - HR department
  - Finance and accounting department
  - IT department

This section discusses, in brief, examples of innovation management programs that would be identified and included in the HR innovation-support strategy for Walu Technologies. There are eleven examples of innovation management programs discussed in this section:

- Translate the meaning of innovation
- Interpret and create dimensions of Innovation
- Formulate organizational innovation goals
- Create innovation roles
- Create innovation-challenge questions
- Innovation-idea management system
- Identifying and hiring innovation talent
- Evaluating innovation performance of workforces
- Innovation talent succession planning
- Measuring and reporting innovation performance

Innovation Priority Areas

What are innovation priority areas (IPAs)? Recall in Chapter One, companies are now making innovation everyone's job across the organization. However, in order to yield meaningful benefits from investments in innovation, it is important to be selective and strategic in terms of areas to focus innovation-support activities on. Therefore, IPAs are organizational activities that are prioritized for innovation. The role of HR, therefore, is to help functional units *identify*, *prioritize*, and *structure* functional-unit areas and activities where innovation should be focused. The objective of IPAs is twofold: (1) to invest in innovation-support activities strategically and (2) to make it easy for workforces to understand where they should focus their innovation-ideation efforts within their functional units and activities.

Steps

1. Outline the core and support functional units.

2. Collaborate and confer with core functional units to identify and structure IPAs in the context of each unit.

3. Create tables for structuring IPAs in the context of each functional unit, starting with core units.

Below are examples of how IPAs would be structured in three core functional units of Walu Technologies. Namely, product development, marketing, and customer service. This is shown in the three tables: 3-1, 3-2, and 3-3.

Table 3-1. Example of structuring product development and processing IPAs

IPAs for product development and processing department	
Software solutions	
Product category	**Time frame for generating innovation ideas**
Software product A	
Software product B	
Software product C	
Cloud storage solutions	
Product category	**Time frame for generating innovation ideas**
Cloud storage product A	
Cloud storage product B	
Cloud storage product C	

Cybersecurity solutions	
Product category	**Time frame for generating innovation ideas**
Cybersecurity product A	
Cybersecurity product B	
Cybersecurity product C	
Date when the outline was done:	
Name and position title of the head of the product segment:	

Table 3-2. Example of structuring marketing IPAs

IPAs for marketing department	
Marketing units IPAs	
Name of unit	**Time frame for generating innovation ideas**
Product pricing	
Product promotion	
Product delivery process	
New markets	
Date when the outline was done:	
Name and position title of the head of department:	

Table 3-3. Example of structuring customer service IPAs

IPAs for customer service department	
Customer service units IPAs	
Name of unit	**Time frame for generating innovation ideas**
Customer service, before purchase unit	
Customer service, during purchase unit	
Customer service, after purchase unit	
Date when the outline was done:	
Name and position title of the head of department:	

Identifying IPAs in Support Functional Units

Usually, innovation ideas generated in support functional units of an organization are aimed at cost-saving and efficiency purposes in the context of the activities of each support functional unit. Assume we want to outline the areas in which innovation should be focused in all the support functional units of Walu Technologies listed below:

- Procurement department
- HR department
- Finance and accounting department
- IT department

Table 3-4 is an example of how IPAs would be structured in a support functional unit. HR must collaborate and confer with all support functional units to identify and structure IPAs in each of the support functional units.

Table 3-4. Example of structuring cost-saving IPAs for procurement

IPAs for procurement department	
Procurement cost-saving IPAs	
Name of unit	Time frame for generating innovation ideas
Procurement component A	
Procurement component B	
Procurement component C	
Procurement component D	
Procurement component E	
Date when the outline was done:	
Name and position title of the head of department:	

Similar tables would be created for the other functional units:

- HR department
- Finance and accounting department
- IT department

Translate the Meaning of Innovation

By its nature, a culture of innovation is not easy to create in an organization. It is even harder for the leadership to get all workforces across the organization engaged in the innovation process if they do not understand what innovation means in the context of the business model and functional activities of the company. In other words, innovation culture in organizations thrives when workforces—leadership included—are able to understand how innovation connects to them (including aligning their success) on personal, professional, and business levels. This requires the translation of innovation terms, concepts, and policies in the corporate language of the company. However, many companies lack this aspect. So translating key innovation concepts and terms including the meaning of innovation into the corporate language of the company is the starting point.

How would individuals get engaged in a process if, to start with, they do not even understand its meaning? For this reason, the second program included in the HR innovation-support strategy is *translating the meaning of innovation*, so that workforces have a clear understanding of what innovation entails in the context of various functional activities of their organization.

Definition of Innovation

This book defines innovation as: *a process that involves identifying a problem or need, generating a new idea that has not been seen on the market before, turning the idea into a solution to address the identified need, and then converting the solution into monetary value.*

HR has two tasks in relation to the above definition:

1. To help the organization formulate and adopt the official meaning of innovation in the context of the organization's business model.

2. To help functional units formulate and adopt the meaning of innovation in the context of their functional activities.

Example

For Walu Technologies, the task of translating the meaning of innovation in the HR innovation-support strategy is for the head of HR (together with HR team undertaking the innovation-support strategy) to collaborate with other department heads and formulate the official definition of innovation reflecting the business model of the company, and as well as each functional unit. For example, the definition of innovation in the context of Walu Technologies would be:

- Identify needs/gaps within the three areas that the company operates: software, cloud storage and cybersecurity.

- Generating innovative product ideas (i.e., ideas never seen in the three spaces before).

- Turn the innovative ideas (through an established process) into solutions (not seen by customers or the market before) to deal with the needs/gaps identified in the three spaces.

- Convert the product solutions into commercial value (i.e., in terms of customer attraction and retention, revenue, competitiveness, and growth).

Creating Sub-Unit Definitions

As mentioned earlier, besides translating the meaning of innovation in the context of the company's business model, it is important to help functional units formulate and adopt the meaning of innovation in the context of their functional activities. To achieve this, HR must collaborate with all functional units to formulate the definition of innovation that workforces will easily understand in the context of the activities within their functional units.

Assuming we are translating the meaning of innovation in the context of all the activities of the core and support functional units of the fictitious company introduced earlier, Walu Technologies, how should it be done? Chapter Nine of *Leadership for Innovation* has a detailed section on how to translate the meaning of innovation in the context of activities of functional units. Please, check it out.

Translate and Create Dimensions of Innovation

The third example of the innovation management program is the concept of *dimensions of innovation*. As mentioned earlier, it is difficult for workforces to relate to the company's call for advancing a culture of innovation if the meaning of innovation is not translated in the context of the work that they do on a daily basis. We have so far discussed the meaning of *innovation* and how the meaning can be translated to fit the context of the organization's business model and functional activities.

So, once you have identified the IPAs and translated the meaning of innovation, it is also important to translate the concept of dimensions of innovation into the organization`s functional unit activities and the business model. The role of HR in this aspect is to lead and coordinate the process of collaborating with other functional units to translate and formulate dimensions of innovation in the context of the business model and functional activities of all the departments.

That being said, what does dimensions of innovation entail? Innovation occurs in different organizational contexts, and these contexts are referred to as *dimensions of innovation*. The term *dimensions of innovation* describe two related innovation concepts in which innovation occurs. These two concepts are *types of innovation* and *innovation degree*. The simple diagram below illustrates the two concepts that relate to dimensions of innovation.

Figure 3-1. Illustration of dimensions of innovation

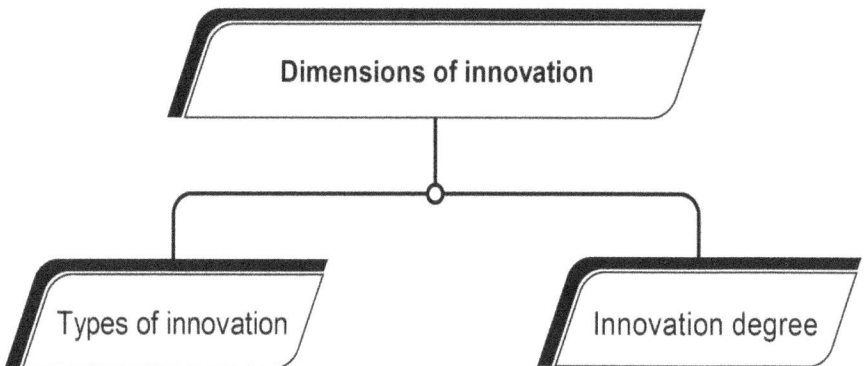

To understand the two concepts let's use a simple analogy of a basket containing a mixture of fruits and veggies of different types, colors, and sizes. How does the basket of veggies and fruits relate to the dimensionality of innovation? Three relations can be highlighted as follows:

- *Variety of fruits and veggies:* This relates to the fact that innovation occurs in the different contexts of the various functional activities and business segments of an organization.

- *Each fruit or veggie has a name:* This relates to the fact that there are different kinds of innovation and that every innovation has a name in the context of a particular aspect of the organization's business model, functional activity, or business segment.

- *Each fruit or veggie has a different nutritional value:* This relates to the fact that every innovation idea is different in terms of the magnitude of newness or extent of inherent impact (i.e., an innovative idea can be radical or incremental).

How does the above analogy relate to a real organization? We return to the functional units of our fictitious company, Walu Technologies.

Core units

- Product development division, comprising the following units:
  - Software segment
  - Cloud storage segment
  - Cybersecurity segment

- Marketing department, comprising the following units:
  - Product pricing
  - Product delivery process
  - Product promotion
  - New markets

- Customer service department

Support units

- Procurement department
- HR department
- Finance and accounting department
- IT department

The HR leadership team at Walu Technologies must ensure:

1. All employees know and understand that innovation occurs in all the core and support functional units.
2. Every innovation has a name (*type of innovation*) in the context of each functional unit activity and business/ product segment.
3. Every innovation idea is different in terms of the magnitude of newness or extent of inherent impact, and this characteristic is called *innovation degree*.
4. An innovative degree characteristic means that an innovative idea can either be *radical* or *incremental*.

Here is a brief description of what *types of innovation* and *innovation degree* entail.

Types of Innovation

The term *types of innovation* relates to the context (*where*) in which innovation occurs in the organization's functional activities. Therefore, it is vital to understand that innovation occurs in a variety of functional activities across the organization. For instance, there are ideas (innovations) in different contexts of product innovations, depending on the nature of an organization's product platforms. There are also process innovation ideas depending on the nature of an organization, and marketing and customer service innovations, and a whole host of service innovations.

How do the types of innovation relate to Walu Technologies? The example (in Table 3-5) outlines how some of the functional unit activities would be translated into the various innovation categories.

Table 3-5. Translation of functional activities into types of innovation

Walu Technologies Categories of types of Innovations	
Product Development Division	
Category of meat products	Type of innovation
Software products	Software innovations
Cloud storage products	Cloud storage innovations
Cybersecurity products	Cybersecurity innovations
Marketing Department	
Category of marketing units	Type of innovation
Product pricing	Product pricing innovations
Product delivery process	Product delivery-process innovations
Product promotion	Product promotion innovations
New markets	New markets for existing products

Notice that we have not included example of a table for creating types of innovation for support functional units such as those for Walu Technologies. Reason being that usually, types of innovation for support functional units are presented in form of cost-saving innovations depending on the context of the activities of each support functional unit. Chapter Eight of the *Leadership for Innovation* has illustrated in detail how to translate functional activities of support functional units into types of innovation.

Innovation Degree

To remind you, dimensions of innovation is an innovation concept used to describe two innovation-related aspects; that is, *where* innovation occurs and *how* it occurs. We have so far talked about *types of innovation*, which entails *where* innovation occurs.

Innovation degree looks at *how* innovation occurs in any form—or type of innovation. The concept of innovation degree is based on the perception that innovative ideas create or add value in varying degrees or extents. Therefore, innovation degree can be defined as: *the perception of the extent of the newness or novelty of an innovative idea.*

Further details favor details on categories of innovation degree are covered in Chapter Eight in *Leadership for Innovation.*

The role of HR in relation to HR innovation-support strategy is to lead and coordinate the process of collaborating with other functional units to explicitly spell out and interpret in simple and clear terms what the concept of innovation degree entails.

Formulate Organizational Innovation Goals

Remember, we have so far discussed three examples of innovation management programs for an HR innovation-support strategy, the fourth example is formulating *organizational innovation goals*. Table 3-6 gives examples of categories of organizational innovation goals.

Table 3-6. Organizational innovation goals

Category of innovation goals	Description of goals
Corporate innovation-support goal	To implement three to four different innovation-support initiatives (in all categories: innovative thinking, innovation engagement, and innovation management) across all functional units and business segments between February and May of 2020.

Innovation-ideation goal	To generate 50 radical and incremental innovative ideas across the organization between May and August of 2020.
Innovation-idea-development goal	To have 10 innovation ideas undergoing development between May and September of 2020.
Innovation-launch goal	To launch or implement 5 innovations between May and November of 2020.
Monetary innovation goals		
Percentage of revenues	**Percentage of savings**	**Percentage of sales from new markets**
5 percent of the overall revenue should come from product innovations launched in the last six months.	3 percent of the overall savings should come from cost-saving innovations implemented in the last six months.	2.5 percent of overall sales (from existing products) should come from new markets discovered in the last six months.

Three reasons how innovation goals are vital in contributing to the culture of innovation:

1. *Innovation goal setting motivates workforces to generate innovative ideas.* In whatever context of performance activities, performance goal setting plays a vital role in driving performance. In fact, numerous behavioral philosophies have linked goal setting to motivation to perform and the realization of the purpose of a particular performance activity. One often-quoted theory is Aristotle's philosophy of final causality- That is, *action caused by a purpose.* For our purpose, we can say, *goal setting can incite action.* Dr. Edwin Locke (1968), an organizational-behavior philosopher, argues that employees are motivated when they have clear performance goals and are provided feedback about their performance.

The question then is, *how does this description apply to innovation goals?* Although the context of this description is generic, the concepts can also be linked to innovation goal setting. This is so because innovation performance is driven by certain factors—such as revenue or profit goals, market-share goals, customer satisfaction goals, functional-unit-performance goals, and so forth—that incite employees to set individual innovation goals and consequently stimulate them to generate innovative ideas to meet their particular innovation-performance goals and ultimately contribute to the functional-unit goals for innovation and overall goals for corporate innovation. Thus, setting goals for functional-unit innovation contributes to inciting and motivating workforces to generate innovative ideas, and in turn, these ideas fuel the advancement of innovation across the organization.

2. *Employees and teams will understand what is expected of them in terms of contributing to innovation.* Related to the first point, goal-setting theory suggests that one of the effective tools for making progress on goals is ensuring that participants in a group with a common goal are clearly aware of what is expected from them as a whole. In terms of innovation, innovation goal setting contributes to ensuring that teams across functional units are clearly aware of the role of their functional units in advancing innovation. This means that teams will not only understand but will also internalize what is expected of them as individuals and also as part of the larger team in advancing the innovation performance of the functional unit.

3. *Determining or measuring innovation performance involves, in large part, setting and reviewing innovation goals.* Hence, functional leaders and employees must understand what innovation goals are and know how to formulate or set innovation goals for various contexts.

How to Create Functional Unit Innovation Goals in Core and Support Functional Units

There are aspects that must be taken into consideration when formulating innovation goals at all levels of the organization. The *Leadership for Innovation* has a detailed description and examples of how to formulate functional unit innovation goals. Further details about how to formulate workforce innovation ideation goals are covered in Chapter Four in my third book, *How to Evaluate Innovation Performance of Workforces*, published in 2020.

As mentioned before, the role of HR is to help functional units and workforces learn how to formulate functional unit innovation goals and workforce innovation ideation goals.

Create Innovation Roles

The fourth example of an innovation management program is formulating the innovation roles or innovation-performance job descriptions and job specifications. Remember, as a way of creating and sustaining a culture of innovation, many organizations are urging all employees to get involved in advancing innovation. However, it's important to understand that innovation performance in organizations does not take place in a vacuum; it's enacted by workforces in the form of performance by undertaking specific innovation-related roles or tasks. This means that if employees are to effectively execute innovation roles, organizational leaders must integrate innovation-related roles in the job descriptions of the employees, However, despite innovation being a known critical factor to the growth and success of a company, many organizations do not include innovation roles in job descriptions of workforces.

By not including innovation-performance roles or not clearly specifying them in employees' job descriptions, the innovation performance of workforces is left to chance, with the hope that they will execute innovation-related activities based on the encouragement and instructions from the leadership team. Such an expectation is dead on arrival! This approach will give zero results in terms of workforce contribution. Isn't it part of the reason why, despite many companies talking about innovation while encouraging their workforces to generate innovative ideas, they still fail to match the level of innovation rhetoric? Innovation-talent potential in many organizations is being hindered because of poorly spelled out innovation roles.

In my work as a workforce innovation trainer-consultant, I have come across many descriptions of innovation roles and job requirements that are wrongly structured or formatted. For instance, look at the structure of the innovation roles and requirements of the job below. This job was advertised by a Silicon Valley based technology company, but the innovation roles are wrongly structured.

Senior Innovation Consultant

Job Overview

As a Senior Innovation Consultant, you will play a pivotal role building a newly launched, transformational division. This highly visible role reports to the Vice President of Innovation, and works closely with early stage innovation consultants, internal business executives and leads the efforts on new programs designed to deliver on our promise of our organizational mission. You'll manage and influence cross-functional project teams, evaluate new technology offerings, lead testing and implementation of pilots, and deliver on product development commitments throughout the aggressive march to roll out solutions.

What you will be doing:

- Work collaboratively with cross-functional teams to bring new and innovative concepts into the company`s ecosystem, with the intent to test, trial and commercialize.
- Evaluate new technologies and collaboration opportunities with stakeholders from throughout the innovation ecosystem (including startups, corporates, academic entities, airline and retail partners and regulatory bodies.)
- Apply appropriate tools and defined methodologies that enable the business to meet customer needs, maintain or grow market share, and ultimately transform the travel industry.
- Coordinate larger and more complex project activities with other business areas to include and identify appropriate stakeholders and coordinating responsibilities across cross functional teams.

- Develop and execute implementation plans while 'owning' program process metrics for prototypes and pilots
- Manage all projects to completion including project schedule, budget, work plan, success metrics, risks and constraints, and appropriate status reporting to assure project activities are delivered in scope, on time and in budget.
- Create business requirements, vendor assessments, specifications, prototype design requirements, and quality assurance measures to advance concepts through the innovation process.

Jon Requirements: What we desire:

- Proven experience managing large, complex B-to-B and/ or B-to-C projects; management of multi-disciplinary teams in a corporate environment.
- High tolerance for ambiguity and experience working to define solutions and maximize business opportunity – must be flexible in approach to solving problems.
- Acute relationship management skills with keen ability to coordinate manage and build relationships with internal and external stakeholders – strong communicator and collaborator.
- Ability to be a self-starter, comfortable with ambiguity and able to work in dynamic, collaborative, and open environment.
- Commitment to act with integrity, be transparent and appropriately inclusive, seek new ways that are right for the business and *get stuff done.*

A poorly or wrongly structured innovation-job profile has a high chance of attracting the wrong job applicants, consequently leading to hiring the wrong candidate with no right mix of innovation skillsets to meet the requirements of the innovation roles of the job under consideration. Also, wrongly structured innovation-job profiles can result in underutilizing innovation skills of jobholders.

Innovation-Performance Job Descriptions

An innovation-performance job description is an outline of innovation-related roles and responsibilities. Understanding the context and formulation of innovation roles is a vital factor. So, innovation roles are separated into three categories, which are: *innovative thinking–related duties and responsibilities, innovation engagement–related duties and responsibilities*, and *innovation management–related duties and responsibilities*. These are interpreted as follows:

- *Innovative thinking–related duties and responsibilities:* These are duties and responsibilities that are centered on the identification of problems/needs and opportunities and the generation of ideas/solutions to deal with the identified challenges and add commercial value to the organization. Note that specific duties and responsibilities vary by organization and by functional unit. In terms of functional units, innovative ideas can be generated in either core or support functional units. Some of the core functional units could include the product-development unit, manufacturing-processes unit, market-strategy-development unit, and customer service unit. Support functional units could include HR, IT, procurement, finance and accounting, corporate affairs, and so forth. Also bear in mind that innovative ideas generated in support functional units are mainly centered on cost-saving ideas.

- *Innovation engagement–related duties and responsibilities:* These are innovation-performance duties and responsibilities that involve the application of various organizational resources to design and implement initiatives on a regular basis, aimed at educating workforces about innovation through informative and inspirational messages and using different communication approaches and techniques.

- *Innovation management–related duties and responsibilities:* These are innovation-performance duties and responsibilities that are focused on the continual design and implementation of various frameworks, strategies, policies, procedures, and action plans that contribute to managing, systemizing, and advancing innovation performance across the functional units of the organization.

Innovation-Performance Job Specifications

Innovation-performance job specifications are the characteristics, abilities, knowledge, and experience needed to perform innovation performance related duties and responsibilities.

There are three categories of innovation-performance job specifications: *innovative thinking, innovation engagement,* and *innovation management.* Here are the brief details of each:

- *Innovative thinking job specifications:* These are the characteristics - knowledge, abilities, and experience required to perform innovative thinking-related duties and responsibilities.
- *Innovation engagement job specifications:* These are the characteristics - knowledge, abilities, and experience required to perform innovation engagement-related duties and responsibilities.
- *Innovation management job specifications*: These are the characteristics - knowledge, abilities, and experience required to perform innovation management-related duties and responsibilities.

Below is an example of a simple template for structuring innovation roles and requirements.

Table 3-7. Categories of innovation performance duties and requirements

Name of department: Position title:		
State whether position title is *limited or generic:*		
If *generic*, indicate number of position titles:		
Three categories of innovation performance roles		
Innovative thinking-related duties and responsibilities	Innovation engagement-related duties and responsibilities	Innovation management-related duties & responsibilities
Categories of innovation performance job requirements		
Innovative thinking abilities	Innovation engagement abilities	Innovation management abilities

It should be spelled out in the HR innovation-support strategy document that the role of HR is to help functional units across the organization formulate innovation roles.

Create Innovation-Challenge Questions

As mentioned, *innovation* is a process that involves four aspects:

1. Identifying a need or problem
2. Generating an innovative idea to fix the identified problem
3. Transforming the innovative idea into a solution not seen on the market before
4. Converting the solution to monetary value.

The relevant part for this section in relation to the above listed aspects is the aspect number one. i.e. ability to identify the needs or problems. Since the goal of the HR innovation-support strategy is to create an environment in which all workforces take part in generating innovative ideas, workforces in all functional units must have the tools for identifying different contexts of problems and needs. So, the fifth example of innovation management program that could be considered for the HR innovation-support strategy is to help functional units to continually formulate innovation-challenge questions in innovation priority areas.

Innovation-challenge questions are pinpointed exploratory questions formulated to reveal specific organizational or community problems/needs or business opportunities requiring innovative solutions. These questions are innovation-related that are strategically formulated, on a continual basis, to reveal a specific need, problem, or opportunity in the context of the organization's value chain or business model. All employees are encouraged to generate innovative ideas that specifically target the characteristics of the identified need, problem, or business opportunity.

Importance of Innovation-Challenge Questions

*   It helps to guide and stimulate workforces to generate focused and pinpointed innovative ideas.

- It encourages workforces to realize innovative thinking potential.
- It promotes the continual flow of different types and degrees of innovative ideas.

Chapter Twelve in *Leadership for Innovation* describes these aspects in detail.

Ensure that Good Innovation-Challenge Questions are Formulated

Generating innovation-challenge questions that can effectively elicit innovative solutions from workforces is paramount to success. HR must coordinate efforts to create sub-committees to formulate innovation-challenge questions. These committees must ensure that every innovation-challenge question that is formulated and publicized to workforces has the ability to elicit effective innovative solutions.

Characteristics of Good Innovation-Challenge Questions

Questions should:

1. Be focused and pinpointed in terms of bringing out the need, problem, or opportunity that requires innovative ideas.
2. Use simple and plain language.
3. Ensure that there is only one innovation-challenge question per need, problem, or opportunity.
4. Be preceded by a brief outline of the factors influencing the need for innovative ideas in a particular functional unit or business/product segment.
5. The innovation-challenge questions should be aligned with the company's corporate innovation language.

Illustration

In this example, a fictitious scenario is used to create an innovation challenge questions worksheet. Environmental Solutions (ES), a fictitious company that specializes in developing innovative environmental solutions, is contracted by the Contra Costa Conservation and Development Unit (CCCDU)—an agency responsible for regulating forestry activities for Contra Costa County of the state of California. Environmental Solutions is expected to help the agency come up with an innovative solution for taking forest inventories.

Current system

Currently, the foresters from the CCCDU take inventories of trees by hiking through representative plots and recording each tree. They extrapolate information from those samples to get the general sense of the land. The bigger and more diverse the forest, the more plots that must be sampled.

The problem

This method has frustrated staff in the CCCDU because the system is inefficient and not very effective. For instance, workers are unable to gather information from ground sampling alone, and the system is very time consuming and uses a lot of workforce power.

Application of innovation-challenge questions

In this case, ES has a director responsible for operations. As a starting point, the director creates an Innovation-Challenge Questions Committee, which is tasked with two goals: (1) Create a forest inventory innovation-challenge-questions worksheet and (2) Formulate (using the worksheet) innovation-challenge questions in the context of a forest inventory. This will stimulate the generation of innovative ideas for creating the forest inventory system.

Table 3-8 provides an example of a forest inventory innovation challenge questions worksheet that could be used in this scenario.

Table 3-8. Innovation-challenge-questions for Forest Inventory Unit

Type of innovation-challenge questions: Forest inventory innovation-challenge questions
Product or service segment: Forest Inventory Unit
Name of innovation-challenge-question committee: Forest Inventory Committee
Date when the innovation-challenge questions were publicized to workforces: April 30, 2020
The table is divided into two parts: Part I is for radical innovation-challenge questions, and Part II is for incremental innovation-challenge questions.
Part I **Innovation degree:** Radical innovation-challenge questions

Describe factors influencing the need for radical innovative ideas for the Forest Inventory Unit	**Context of the radical innovation-challenge questions: Forest Inventory Unit**	
• The current system is inefficient and not very effective. • The Forest Inventory Unit is unable to get information from ground sampling alone. • The current system requires a lot of work.	***Radical innovation-challenge question:*** *What radical forest inventory solution/method would help the Forest Inventory Unit to undertake the inventory tasks in the following list?*	
	1. Tally the sizes of the trees in a more efficient and effective manner	
	2. Tally the number of trees in a more efficient and effective manner	
	3. Identify and tally the species of the trees in a more efficient and effective manner	

	4. Locate the ideal mushroom habitat
	5. Complete items 1–4 with less manpower
	6. Establish a system that will also result in the creation of detailed inventories to help maximize timber yields

Part II
Innovation degree: Incremental innovation-challenge questions

Describe factors influencing the need for the generation of incremental innovative ideas for the Forest Inventory Unit	Incremental innovation-challenge questions
• The current system is inefficient and not very effective. • The Forest Inventory Unit is unable to get information from ground sampling alone. • The current system involves a lot of work.	*What incremental forest inventory solutions/ ideas would help the Forest Inventory Unit to undertake the inventory tasks in the following list?*
	1. Tally the sizes of the trees in a more efficient and effective manner
	2. Tally the number of trees in a more efficient and effective manner
	3. Identify and tally the species of the trees in a more efficient and effective manner
	4. Locate the ideal mushroom habitat
	5. Complete items 1–4 with less manpower

Time frame for submission of forest inventory innovative ideas from Environmental Solutions after publication of the forest inventory innovation-challenge questions: One month
Innovation-challenge-questions status report: The committee is expected to submit a status report noting the following: • Number of forest inventory innovation-challenge questions formulated within the prescribed time period   • Number of forest inventory innovative ideas generated as a result of the forest inventory innovation-challenge questions publicized to Environmental Solutions staff
Names and positions of subcommittee members:

Chapter Twelve in *Leadership for Innovation* describes in detail how to manage innovation-challenge questions and also provides worksheets for creating innovation challenge questions in functional units and product segments of an organization.

HR should ensure that every functional unit develops frameworks for creating innovation challenge questions in the context of their functional activities.

Innovation-idea Management System

It's often said that human progress depends on ideas. While the accuracy of this statement is indisputable—clearly, it is important to bear in mind that unless they are developed, ideas cannot bring about human progress. In short, raw ideas cannot bring about human advancement. In order to harness ideas to bring about human development, ideas have to be developed, and at the core of the aspect of idea-development should be an effective assessment process to ensure that only ideas with a high potential for generating the intended results are developed. In the context of an organization, one could say that although the growth of any organization depends on ideas, unless they are developed into something that adds value to the organization's cause, by themselves, innovation ideas cannot grow or advance an organization. As the old saying goes, "Clever business ideas that cannot be commercialized are nothing more than dead trees."

Having an effective management system for innovation ideas is one of the most critical tools for sustaining a successful culture of innovation. What this means is that without the ability and institutional capability to translate the ideas into solutions converted into monetary value, the whole mission of advancing innovation or creating a culture of innovation will be rendered unattainable.

So, the sixth example of innovation management program that should be included in the HR innovation-support strategy is creating an effective innovation-idea management system for managing innovation-ideas generated across functional units.

Definition

An innovation-idea management system is defined as an organizational process that involves creating tools, techniques, and procedures for assessing and developing, on a continual basis, innovative ideas gathered across all functional units into solutions that contribute monetary value to the organization.

Designing and Implementing the Innovation-Idea Management System

The innovation-idea management system has a lot of moving parts. Developing a system aimed at scaling ideation across all functional units requires approaches that will manage large volumes of diverse ideas across the organization.

Each functional unit or business segment must have a robust and effective system for gathering and managing innovation ideas within the context of the functional unit's activities. Chapter Fourteen in *Leadership for Innovation* describes in detail how to design and implement a company-wide innovation-idea management system.

What kind of aspects should one include in the organization's innovation-idea management framework to make it implementable and effective? Here is an example of an innovation-idea management framework.

Figure 3-2. Innovation-idea management framework

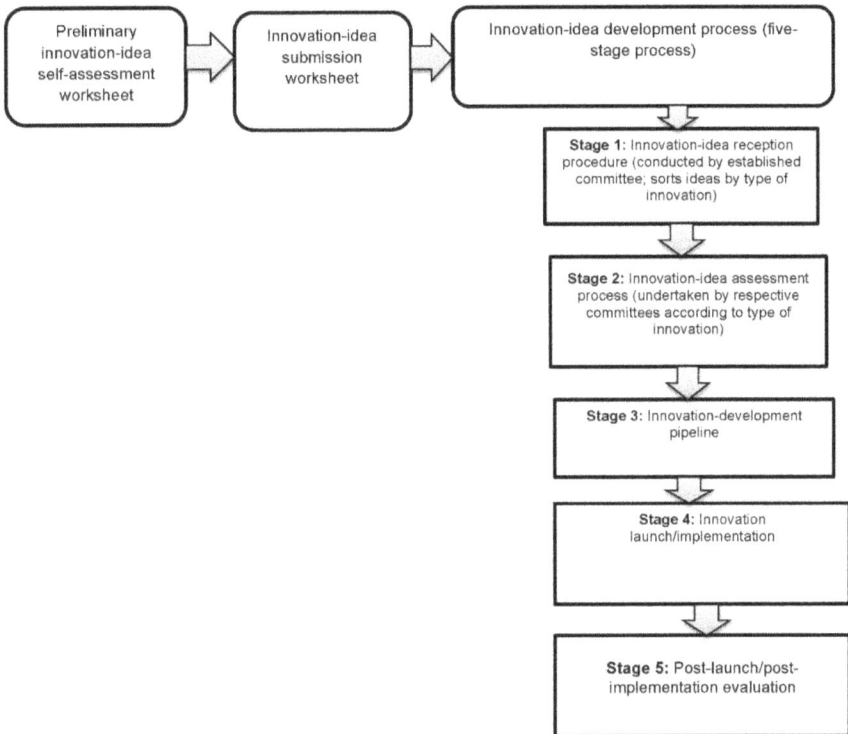

Adapted from, *Leadership for Innovation*, 2020

Chapter Fourteen in *Leadership for Innovation* describes in detail how each of the stages or tools outlined in figure 3-2 can be implemented.

Identifying and Hiring Innovation Talent

Remember, creating and sustaining a culture of innovation requires a great deal of innovation-related interventions in terms of policies, strategies, and practices. It does not happen naturally.

We have so far looked at six examples of innovation management programs. One of the vital elements for sustaining a culture of innovation is having a mix of innovation talent. There are many pathways of building innovation talent across functional units, one of the pathways is recruitment of innovation talent. However, talent recruitment per say does not provide innovation talent because you cannot hire innovation talent using non-innovation oriented traditional talent recruitment methods and tools. That's where this section comes in.

So, the seventh innovation management program is implementing an effective system for hiring innovation talent. The head of HR should ensure that the HR innovation-support strategy includes activities aimed at helping every functional unit with the implementation tools and approaches for identifying and hiring the right mix of innovation talent for both experienced and entry level hires. The question is, what tools and steps should an organization implement in order to hire job candidates with the right mix of innovation skill sets? My book, *Hiring for Innovation,* 2020 provides an easy to read and apply steps and tools for creating company-wide mechanism for identifying innovation skills and competencies in job candidates.

Evaluating Innovation Performance of Workforces

The eighth innovation management program is a mechanism for evaluating innovation performance of workforces. Studies and analysts on innovation agree that workforce performance trends are shifting away from "routine work" and toward innovation performance. Many companies are implementing practices aimed at creating a culture of innovation.

However, innovation performance practices do not occur naturally, a system has to be adopted and practiced. One of the vital ingredients for adopting innovation performance practices that meaningfully contribute to sustaining a culture of innovation is by implementing a company-wide framework to evaluate innovation performance of workforces. Unfortunately, many companies still rely on traditional staff performance appraisals to drive innovation performance practices across functional units. Like a square peg in a round hole, traditional staff appraisals do not produce innovation performance results. So, it is important to ensure that evaluating innovation performance of workforces is adopted companywide.

My third book, *How to Evaluate Innovation Performance of Workforces,* (2020) provides steps and tools for creating a company-wide mechanism for evaluating and rewarding innovation performance of workforces on a continual basis.

Innovation Talent Succession Planning

For more than ten years, I have been engaged in workforce innovation. I've interacted with many organizational leaders on the topic of workforce innovation. I've conducted reviews of studies and publications on the topic of workforce innovation.

My experience is that while most organizational leaders acknowledge that understanding current and future innovation talent needs of the organization is critical in creating and sustaining a culture of innovation, many organizations do not seem to have the necessary tools for creating a mechanisms to monitor their current and future innovation talent. In other words, most organizations do not have the tools to create an organizational framework that ensures that the organization has workforces with a mix of innovation skill sets to meet the current and future innovation performance needs.

To this end, the ninth innovation management program is implementing a mechanism for creating a company-wide innovation talent succession plan. And this program should be included in the HR Innovation-support strategy on a continual basis. My fourth book, *Innovation Talent Succession Planning, 2020* provides steps and tools for creating a pool of workforces with the right mixture of innovation skill sets so that innovation performance of functional units and achievement of short or long-term innovation goals is not negatively affected in case of innovation talent departures.

Measuring and Reporting Innovation Performance

The tenth example of innovation management program is adopting a framework aimed at helping organizational leaders for measuring and reporting innovation performance in the context of an organization's functional activities and business model.

When I conduct training on measuring innovation performance, I sometimes ask participants to indicate by a show of hands if their companies have mechanisms for measuring and reporting innovation performance at the functional-unit level, divisional level, or corporate level. I have never gotten more than five hands in the affirmative out of a group of anywhere from twenty-five to forty people. Interestingly, when I ask them to indicate whether innovation is considered a top-three priority in their organizations, 90–95 percent raise their hands. Studies by Boston Consulting Group and Institute for Corporate Productivity, two US-based consulting firms, reveal that many companies do not track innovation performance as rigorously as other business elements, creating an ongoing challenge on how to measure and report innovation performance.

My fifth book, *How to Measure and Report Innovation Performance*, defines *innovation-performance measurement* as a process that involves reviewing and assessing various innovation performance–related activities at the functional-unit and corporate levels, then determining goals that have been met, based on various aspects of innovation activities that have been achieved. Chapter Five, Step Two of this book outlines the importance of measuring innovation performance in relation to determining the efficacy of the HR innovation-support strategy. The question is, how do you measure innovation performance?

Here are four metrics for measuring innovation performance:

- Innovation input measurement
- Innovation output measurement
- Innovation-results measurement
- Innovation impact measurement

These are described in detail in Step Two of Chapter Five of the above mentioned book.

Category B: Innovative Thinking Programs

As mentioned at the beginning of this chapter, this book has suggested three categories of innovation-support programs that are essential for developing and implementing an HR innovation-support strategy, namely:

- Category A: Innovation management programs
- Category B: Innovative thinking programs
- Category C: Innovation engagement programs

We`ve so far discussed *category A*. The second category is *innovative thinking programs*.

To understand what innovative thinking programs entail, it is important to start with the meaning of innovative thinking. To do this, we begin with the definition of an *innovative person*. An innovative person is one who possesses abilities and characteristics that drive innovative performance. The next question would then be, *what is innovative performance?*

Innovative performance can be defined as an expression of innovative thinking abilities in response to a need or problem in the context of an organization's functional activity. To understand this perspective of the meaning of innovative thinking, take a look at the following IBM story.

A senior executive at IBM contributed to building a Life Sciences Unit at the company. Anne Robertson (not her real name) was in charge of a unit she had built from scratch to its current status of more than two thousand employees. Robertson learned that her mother had developed complications during a health treatment when she reacted adversely to a particular medication. Although Anne's mother's records were updated to warn doctors not to repeat the treatment, just three days later, another doctor missed that warning and gave her the very same medicine. Robertson was shocked when she found out how common and widespread the problem was in US hospitals. According to reports, more than 100,000 people die every year in US hospitals because of medical errors such as incorrect medication, incorr ect dosage, inefficient diagnostics, duplicated procedures, operations on the wrong side of the body, and so forth; and the problem has been going on for many years. Robertson started thinking about how IBM could solve the problem in an innovative way or in a way not seen on the market before. Today, IBM's Life Sciences Unit manufactures and supplies IT systems that are helping hospitals manage their patient data more effectively.

This IBM story illustrates the connection between noticing a *problem* and generating an *innovative idea*, which, in essence, is an expression of innovative performance.

Importance

Based on the definition of innovative thinking, why is it important to include innovative thinking programs in the HR innovation-support strategy? Two reasons:

1. In order to create a culture of innovation, innovative thinking must be a crosscutting practice within the company. To scale the practice of innovative thinking across the organization, one vital aspect that the head of HR has to clarify and instill in the hearts and minds of both the top leadership and all the workforces is that innovative thinking is not an area

reserved for specific persons or functional units. That is, innovative thinking is a skill that all employees can attain or develop, regardless of their level in the organizational structure or functional unit under which they fall. Therefore, the inclusion of innovative thinking programs in the HR innovation-support strategy.

2. Understanding what innovative thinking entails helps everyone in the organization to interpret how innovative thinking skills can be expressed and applied in the context of the company's corporate innovation language. According to the *Human Capital Trends—2012* report by Deloitte LLP, many companies are now defining *innovation* broadly to include such aspects as services, processes, business models, communication, and cost-structure improvements across the enterprise. Thus, understanding innovative thinking skills helps both leaders and workforces to interpret how innovative thinking abilities can be applied and expressed across the various functional activities and business segments of the company.

Approaches for Developing Innovative Thinking Abilities

It must be noted that one of the reasons for implementing innovative thinking programs is twofold: (1) to educate personnel that innovative thinking is a skill or an ability that can be attained and applied by anyone in the organization, (2) to explore workforces to various tools for developing innovative thinking skills. There's a long-held view of experts in the fields of psychology and innovation is that humans have billions of brain cells and great creative capacity. Implying that, generally, people have an amazing potential for innovative thinking; however, most people do not automatically have the ability to tap into the brain's creative and innovative potential. This is the reason for including programs and approaches that focus on programs aimed at helping workforces develop innovative thinking abilities. The question, then, becomes, *what approaches can be applied to develop innovative thinking skills and the ability to tap into innovative potential?* Here is a list of some examples of approaches for building innovative thinking skills or abilities:

- Associating attribute
- Questioning attribute
- Observing attribute
- Experimenting attribute
- Networking attribute
- Envisioning attribute
- Problem-solving attribute
- No fear-for-failure attribute
- Risk-taking attribute
- Challenging-status-quo attribute
- Grit attribute
- Thinking time attribute

Chapter Two of *Leadership for Innovation* describes in detail how most of the attributes listed above can be developed, thereby, enhancing or contributing to one's innovative thinking ability.

HR should include programs, initiatives, and activities in the HR innovation-support strategy to help workforces across functional units develop or enhance most of their innovative thinking attributes.

Importance of organizational leaders to have innovative thinking abilities in leading a culture of innovation

As stated before, creating and sustaining a culture of innovation depends on many organizational leadership factors.

One key factor is that organizational leaders must lead by example in driving innovation. So, the HR innovation-support strategy must educate leaders across the organization that it is vitally important for them to be seen by their followers exhibiting meaningful degrees of innovative thinking. Based on the importance of leaders in cultivating innovative thinking across workforces, it is important for HR to develop a lot of innovative thinking initiatives for the company's leaders.

Let's dive into this subject of leading by example a little bit. According to the old and common cliché in leadership, "Leadership is by example." The application of this adage is that for a leader to expect a particular behavior from followers, the leader must be seen to exhibit the same, or even better, behavior that he or she expects from followers. Studies in leadership by example, also referred to as *leadership role modeling*, have revealed that in most cases, followers will demonstrate a particular behavior demanded of them by their leaders only if they see their leaders displaying a similar behavior. In other words, followers learn through emulation or imitation. For instance, if you, as a leader, emphasize the behavior of good time management to your teams, you must lead by excelling in observing task deadlines so that your followers can emulate you.

Similarly, if you champion a culture of cost saving, you've got to lead by example by being the first one to stay on budget. In simple terms, you cannot champion a behavior or culture that you don't exhibit yourself and expect your followers to adopt it. One of the most widely quoted aphorisms of Mahatma Gandhi is as follows: "What we do and what we say must be in alignment." In a basic sense, the essence of leadership by example is about setting standards in collaboration with followers and, in turn, leading followers in embracing and exhibiting the set standards.

Category C: Innovation Engagement Programs

It said that innovation is a mind-set that should pervade the entire organization. The third and final category of the innovation-support program is *innovation engagement programs*. Sentiments indicating that innovation is a hearts-and-minds process have been expressed by many innovation experts and analysts. However, one aspect rarely emphasized is the issue of tools for helping workforces instill innovation in their hearts and minds. It is important to understand that pervasiveness of innovation in the hearts and minds of workforces is not a natural occurrence; it requires consistent implementation of programs, activities, and approaches aimed at building workforce engagement in advancing innovation. This is by no means an easy task. It requires implementing specific innovation-related programs for securing employee engagement in innovation. For this reason, the HR innovation-support strategy should include a range of programs and initiatives aimed at instilling in the hearts and minds of workforces. Since innovation engagement programs are a key component of the HR innovation-support strategy, we will give an elaborate description of what innovation engagement entails.

Definition

The term innovation engagement programs refers to an integrated range of *informative* and *inspirational* styles and organizational activities aimed at instilling innovation in the hearts and minds of workforces.

Stated broadly, innovation engagement programs involve development and implementation of different kinds of programs and activities, on a regular basis, for the following purposes:

- Educating workforces about what various aspects and concepts of innovation entail in the context of the company`s corporate language.
- Inspiring and instilling innovation in the hearts and minds of workforces so that workforces are meaningfully engaged in terms of building passion for, commitment to, and emotional interest in advancing innovation across the organization.
- Publicizing the various innovation-support strategies and systems implemented or intended to be implemented by the organization.

- Educating workforces about the significance of innovation to achieving corporate growth and long-term competitiveness of the organization, the impact of innovation on the economic well-being of communities, and the influence of innovation on the career development of workforces.

Communication Styles

The innovation engagement involves implementing diverse hearts and minds activities that are delivered in two different communication styles: *informative* and *inspirational*.

Description of Informative and Inspirational Styles

Informative Style

This style involves instilling innovation in the hearts and minds of workforces by informing them (through various communication options) on a regular basis about the innovation-support systems—such as innovation strategies, innovation policies, innovation procedures, innovation goals, and innovation plans—that the organization intends to implement or has implemented to advance innovation across the organization. It also involves crosscutting communication by leadership about the innovation performance of various functional units or divisions of the organization and the whole organization.

Inspirational Style

This style involves the continual use of innovation-motivating slogans, catchphrases, and visual illustrations to instill passion for and emotional interest in innovation in the hearts and minds of workforces. The inspirational style aims to achieve two things: (1) to influence workforces to believe in and understand wholeheartedly the importance of innovation to the competitiveness and growth of the organization (and also to their career advancement), and

(2) to instill in the hearts and minds of the workforces a can-do attitude regarding the development of innovative thinking abilities. How is this done? By regularly communicating to workforces the inspirational message that nobody is born with innovative thinking abilities—rather, they are attained, and anybody can learn the innovative thinking skills.

Example of Expressing Informative and Inspirational Styles

From a nonbusiness perspective, one illustration that gives a good depiction of the use or characterization of the informative and inspirational styles is a comparison of speeches by two former US presidents, Bill Clinton and Barack Obama, at the Democratic National Convention (DNC) in September 2012. These two leaders delivered their speeches on different days; both speeches were great, but they had different styles. Clinton delivered his speech on Wednesday, September 5, and Obama delivered his on Thursday, September 6. What is interesting about the speeches is how the two leaders rallied the huge audience at the venue and the viewers across the US to re-elect President Obama.

In his speech, Clinton made a case for President Obama by constantly quoting qualitative and quantitative data on what President Obama had achieved during his first four-year term. In his speech, Clinton articulated the following points:

- What Obama's economic recovery policies had achieved.
- Obama's plans for advancing innovation across sectors.
- The number of jobs created by the Obama administration, including the number of manufacturing jobs, which had been low for the previous decade
- Obama's national educational policies, which focused on preparing young people for twenty-first-century jobs and student loan reforms.

- Obama's energy-sector policies.
- The five-point benefits of Obama's health-care insurance reforms, including clarifications on some of Obama's health-care policies, such as the savings created by Obama's Medicare plan.
- Medicare and Medicaid policy contrasts between Obama and the then Republican presidential nominee, Governor Mitt Romney.
- Highlights of Obama's debt-reduction plan versus Romney's plan.

Thus, Clinton's approach would be considered an informative style. In contrast, President Obama made the case for his re-election to the DNC audience and the American voters through the constant use of motivational and catchphrases centered on words and phrases such as *hope, change, aspirations, opportunity for all, the American Dream*, and *the unwavering character of Americans*. Some examples of the motivational phrases in Obama's DNC speech are as follows:

- "With hope, American problems can be solved."
- "America can make it as long as we don't waver."
- "You have the choice to go backward or move forward with me."
- "You can choose the right future for America."
- "You can choose leadership that is proven and tested."
- "Our efforts must not waver."
- "Change must be defined by the hopes and aspirations of the people."

Application of Informative and Inspirational Styles

The question is, how are informative and inspirational styles applied to instill innovation in the hearts and minds of workforces?

Informative style: The informative style can be applied with the following actions:

- Explaining and articulating how innovation is linked to the overall corporate strategy of the organization.
- Articulating functional-unit innovation goals.
- Explaining and articulating how the innovation-performance goals of each functional unit are aligned with the functional-unit strategy.
- Explaining and articulating how innovation strategies are being implemented across functional units.
- Articulating other innovation-related systems and practices, such as innovation-idea-development procedures, innovation-challenge questions, and various strategies and policies for innovation talent (e.g., innovation talent-recruitment policies, innovation-performance reward policies, talent-diversity policies, innovation talent-succession planning).
- Articulating the number of innovation ideas generated, innovation ideas undergoing development, and innovations launched by various functional units.
- Articulating and explaining the frameworks for innovation-performance reporting that the organization has adopted.
- Articulating the impact of innovation on the performance of the company over a given period.

Inspirational style: In the context of leading workforce innovation, the inspirational style is applied through the use of motivating slogans, catchphrases, and visual illustrations focused on various aspects of innovation, such as the following:

- How innovation is critical to realizing the organization's vision.
- Remind workforces about their potential to generate innovative ideas.

- Meaning of innovation.
- Dimensions of innovation and how this should inspire workforces to generate innovative ideas (i.e. since workforces will understand the organization's broad characterization of innovation)
- Significance of innovation.
- Constantly articulating how innovation performance can drive the organization to greater heights, including examples of companies that have used innovation to transform their business model and achieve unprecedented growth.
- How innovation can propel the careers of workforces to greater heights.

When outlining informative and inspirational styles as actionable activities in the HR innovation-support strategy, HR should ensure that each of the two styles has separate action plans: (i.e. innovation engagement action plan for: *informative activities* and *inspirational activities)*. An application of the informative and inspirational styles in the context of championing a culture of innovation is as follows:

Examples of Expressing Informative and Inspirational Styles

There are two approaches for applying both informative and inspirational styles as a way of expressing innovation engagement programs:

- Use of innovation-motivating slogans and catchphrases
- Use of visual illustrations

Details of the two approaches are as follows:

Use of Innovation-Motivating Slogans and Catchphrases

Instilling innovation in the hearts and minds of workforces is not easy because it requires the application of different forms of approaches and techniques. Whatever the technique that you use, it has to be creative and have a high chance of effectiveness. One of the inspirational techniques is harnessing the power of motivational slogans. Great slogans are memorable, and they captivate people's emotional interest and passion in relation to the intended context or purpose. Thus, innovation-motivating slogans are one of the effective techniques for instilling innovation engagement in the hearts and minds of workforces to sustain a culture of innovation. However, not every innovation slogan or catchphrase is effective in terms of instilling innovation in the hearts and minds. To formulate effective slogans and catchphrases certain aspects should be considered. The following are some of the characteristics of good innovation-motivating slogans:

- *Use simple and emotionally connecting language:* Innovation-motivating slogans should be written in simple, creative language and should have the potential to stimulate an emotional connection in the hearts of workforces. An example of an innovation-motivating catchphrase with less of an emotional effect could be written as follows:

   "Lack of innovation weakens the competitiveness of our company."

   On the other hand, the following innovation catchphrase will potentially have a stronger emotional effect on the hearts and minds of workforces than the first one:

   "Lack of innovation creates a laid-back culture, laid-back products, and a laid-back company. And a laid-back company cannot be competitive!"

- *Workforces should be able to form pictures or images from the message:* You should ensure that workforces are able to form visual images from the innovation-motivating slogans. Remember, because slogans consist only of words, without visual illustrations, innovation-motivating slogans should allow workforces to create visual images from the words used. Here is an example:

"Our company lives on ocean waves: without innovation, we're tossed!"

- *Reflect the context of the message used:* Ensure that you create innovation-motivating slogans that reflect the context of the intended innovation message that you are trying to communicate. For instance, slogans centered on the connection between innovation and the organizational vision, revenues, profits, competitiveness, career development, and so forth should clearly reflect this context.

- *Use impacting language:* Innovation-motivating slogans are intended to enculturate various aspects of innovation in the hearts and minds of workforces. Ensure that the language expressed in the slogans enables workforces to ingrain the intended aspects of innovation in their hearts and minds. For example:

  "Innovation is the sailboat of the vision of our company."

- *Illuminate benefits in simple and creative terms:* If you are trying to communicate the benefits of innovation, ensure that the innovation-motivating slogans make clear, in simple and creative ways, the benefits of innovation to the company, communities, and workforces.

Here are some examples of channels for communicating innovation-motivating slogans.

- Plaques inscribed with innovation-motivating slogans or catchphrases
- Innovation-motivating slogans on company uniforms
- Monitors displaying innovation-motivating slogans
- Innovation-motivating slogans on calendars
- Innovation-motivating posters
- Innovation-motivating slogans on pens
- Other channels include mugs, bags, T-shirts, etc.

Use of Visual Illustrations

The second technique for communicating or publicizing innovation engagement messages is the use of visual illustrations.

Definition

The promotion of innovation through visual illustration is a technique that involves the use of simple visual art, pictures, or any type of drawing to communicate a particular context of innovation to workforces with the intention of (1) educating workforces about a specific aspect of innovation, (2) instilling the message of the importance of innovation to the company, communities, and workforces in the hearts and minds of those workforces, and (3) instilling the spirit of innovative thinking in the hearts and minds of workforces.

Importance of Visual Illustration

The use of visual illustration as one of the effective techniques for educating workforces about aspects of innovation and instilling the importance of innovation in the hearts and minds of those workforces is based on the idea that visual communication has a greater power to inform, educate, persuade, captivate, and motivate people to get involved and support a particular cause. Numerous studies have been conducted on the impact of visual illustrations on productivity. For instance, a study by the University of St. Gallen in Switzerland showed high productivity in managers who used a lot of visual illustration techniques to communicate various organizational activities to workforces compared with managers who did not use visual illustration techniques.

Types of Visual Illustration Techniques

A number of techniques can be applied to communicate or promote visual messages about innovation across the organization. Example of the techniques include the use of:

- Signs
- Pictures
- Drawings
- Graphic designs
- Electronic resources, such as monitors displaying different kinds of innovation-related visual illustrations

The above aspects can be used in different forms to depict, convey, or communicate a particular context of innovation.

- The following are some of the examples of the aspects of innovation that can be communicated across functional units with the use of visual illustrations:
- Visual illustrations on the connection between innovation and increases in revenues and profits, growth, competitiveness, and career development for workforces
- Visual illustrations on the meaning of *innovation*
- Visual illustrations on the significance of innovation
- Visual illustrations on types of innovation in the context of the organization's business model
- Visual illustrations on the meaning of *innovation degree* (radical innovations and incremental innovations)
- Visual illustrations on various external trends driving the need to advance and sustain innovation performance in the company
- Visual illustrations about the company's innovation vision
- Visual illustrations of functional-unit and corporate innovation goals and targets
- Visual illustrations of the company's innovation policies and practices, such as the following:
  - Funding for innovation R&D
  - Innovation skills development
  - Rewards and recognition policies

- Innovation performance measurements and reporting framework
- Innovation talent succession planning
- Framework for evaluating innovation performance of workforces
- The innovation-idea development process
- The innovation-idea submission process
- Innovation strategies

Part II: Prioritization of Innovation-Support Programs

Before we dive into the details of this section, let's do a recap of Part I. Remember, Chapter Three is segmented into Part I and II. We have so far discussed Part I, which looks at *identifying innovation-support programs* that should be adopted for the HR innovation-support strategy.

As the subtitle suggests, Part II looks at how to prioritize innovation-support programs for purposes of implementing the HR innovation-support strategy across the organization. We have discussed the three categories of innovation-support programs that should be leveraged to develop and implement an HR innovation-support strategy across functional units. The three categories are:

- Category A: Innovation management programs
- Category B: Innovation engagement programs
- Category C: Innovative thinking programs

Prioritization of innovation-support programs or activities is a process that involves deciding the order by which the innovation-support programs or activities should be undertaken for the purposes of the HR innovation-support strategy.

Innovation-Support Priority Scale

A simple tool to help determine priority of innovation-support programs should be created by the HR team that is driving the HR innovation-support strategy. Table 2-5, below, is an example of the *innovation-support priority scale*. The simple rating scale can be used to decide the order by which the innovation-support programs or activities shall be implemented.

Table 3-9. Innovation-support prioritization scale

Category of innovation-support program:				
Specific program or activity:				
Program rating				
1	2	3	4	5
High priority				Low priority
State why the program or activity is categorized high priority:				
State why the program or activity is categorized low priority:				

In collaboration with other heads of functional units and support of the CEO, the head of HR should lead the team responsible for innovation-support strategy to determine the order by which the innovation-support programs or activities will be undertaken. If contextually applicable, you could also establish innovation-support prioritization committee(s) to determine the order of the innovation-support program-priorities.

Illustration: Innovation-Support Program-Priority Listing

Once the rating is determined, the next activity is to indicate the rating of each program in the innovation-support program-priority listing tables. There are two steps. First, create a list of categories with innovation-support programs as follows:

Category A: Innovation Management Programs

- Innovation priority areas
- Translating the meaning of innovation
- Interpreting and creating dimensions of innovation
- Formulating organizational innovation goals
- Creating innovation roles
- Creating innovation-challenge questions
- Innovation-idea management system
- Identifying and hiring innovation talent
- Innovation talent succession planning
- Measuring and reporting innovation performance

Category B: Innovative Thinking Programs

Aimed at equipping workforces with the following innovative thinking attributes:

- Questioning attribute
- Associating attribute
- Experimenting attribute
- Networking attribute
- Envisioning attribute
- No fear-of-failure attribute
- Risk-taking attribute
- Challenging-status-quo attribute
- Grit attribute
- Thinking time attribute
- Educating managers about the importance of role-modeling in leading a culture of innovation

Category C: Innovation Engagement Programs

There are two types of innovation engagement styles: *informative* and *inspirational* style

Informative style: Educating workforces about the company's innovation strategies, practices, policies and procedures such as:

- Link between innovation and overall corporate strategy of the organization
- Functional unit innovation goals
- Corporate innovation goals
- Innovation-idea development system
- Innovation-challenge questions
- Innovation performance measurement and reporting system
- Innovation talent recruitment policy
- Workforce innovation performance evaluation policy

Inspirational style: The use of innovation-motivating slogans, catchphrases, and visual illustrations to educate workforces about various aspects of innovation, such as the following:

- Meaning of innovation.
- Dimensions of innovation.
- Significance of innovation.
- How innovation is critical to realizing the organization's vision.
- Remind workforces about their potential to generate innovative ideas.
- How innovation performance can drive the organization to greater heights, including examples of companies that have used innovation to transform their business model and achieve unprecedented growth.
- How innovation can propel the careers of workforces to greater heights.

Second, create innovation-support program-priority listing tables as shown below. The tables are separated according to the three categories of the innovation-support programs:

- Category A: Innovation management program-priority listing (table 3-10)
- Category B: Innovative thinking program-priority listing (table 3-11)
- Category C: Innovation engagement program-priority listing (table 3-12)

Category A: Innovation Management Program-Priority Listing

This category would be outlined as follows:

Table 3-10. Example of the innovation management program-priority listing

Category A: Innovation management priority programs				
Date when the listing was created:				
Innovation management program	Order of priority (1-5, one being highest)	Scale of the program		Objective of the program or activity
		Limited to Specific functional unit	Crosscutting (implemented in all factional units)	
Innovation priority areas	#1		Crosscutting	To identify innovation priority areas across all functional units and business / product segments
Interpreting and creating dimensions of Innovation	#1		Crosscutting	[Objectives related to each of the other programs would be formulated]

Translating the meaning of innovation	#1		Crosscutting	
Formulating organizational innovation goals	#1		Crosscutting	
Creating innovation roles	#2		Crosscutting	
Creating innovation-challenge questions	#2		Crosscutting	
Innovation-idea management system	#1		Crosscutting	
Identifying and hiring innovation talent	#2		Crosscutting	
Innovation talent succession planning	#3		Crosscutting	
Measuring and reporting innovation performance	#2		Crosscutting	

Category B: Innovative Thinking Program-Priority Listing

This category would be outlined as follows.

Table 3-11. Example of the innovative thinking program-priority listing

Category B: Innovative thinking priority programs				
Date when the listing was created:				
Innovative thinking program (Educating workforces on approaches for developing innovative thinking abilities)	Order of priority (1-5, one being highest)	Scale of the program		Objective of the program or activity
		Limited to Specific functional unit	Crosscutting (implemented in all factional units)	
Questioning attribute	#1		Crosscutting	To equip and enhance questioning abilities in workforces across functional units
Associating attribute	#1		Crosscutting	[Objectives related to each of the other innovative thinking activities would be formulated]
Observing attribute	#1		Crosscutting	
Experimenting attribute	#2		Crosscutting	
Networking attribute	#2		Crosscutting	

Envisioning attribute	#2		Crosscutting	
Problem-solving attribute	#2		Crosscutting	
No fear-of-failure attribute	#2		Crosscutting	
Risk-taking attribute	#2		Crosscutting	
Challenging-status-quo attribute	#1		Crosscutting	
Grit attribute	#2		Crosscutting	
Thinking time attribute	#1		Crosscutting	
Educating managers about the importance of role-modeling in leading a culture of innovation	#1		Crosscutting	

Category C: Innovation Engagement Program-Priority Listing

This category would be outlined as follows. Remember, there are two types of innovation engagement styles *(informative and inspirational)*. So, Table 3-12 is separated into the two types of innovation engagement styles.

Table 3-12. Innovation engagement program-priority listing

Category C: Innovation engagement priority programs *(informative and inspirational styles)*				
Informative Style				
Involves educating workforces about the company's innovation strategies, practices, policies, and procedures				
Date when the listing was created:				
Innovation engagement program	**Order of priority** *(1-5, one being highest)*	**Scale of the program**		**Objective of the program or activity**
		Limited to Specific functional unit	**Crosscutting** (to be implemented in all factional units)	
Link between innovation and overall corporate strategy of the organization	#2		Crosscutting	To educate workforces across functional units about the link between innovation and overall corporate strategy of the organization

Functional unit innovation goals	#1		Crosscutting	[Objectives related to each of the other innovation engagement programs or activities would be formulated]
Corporate innovation goals	#1		Crosscutting	
Innovation-idea development system	#1		Crosscutting	
Innovation-challenge questions	#2		Crosscutting	
Innovation performance measurement and reporting system	#1		Crosscutting	
Innovation talent recruitment policy	#2		Crosscutting	
Innovation talent succession planning	#2		Crosscutting	

Inspirational Style

Involves the use of innovation-motivating slogans, catchphrases, and visual illustrations to educate workforces about various aspects of innovation

Date when the listing was created:				
Innovation engagement program or activity	**Order of priority** *(1-5, one being highest)*	**Scale of the program**		**Objective of the program or activity**
		Limited to Specific functional unit	**Crosscutting** (to be implemented in all factional units)	
Educate workforces about the meaning of innovation in different contexts of the organizations	#2		Crosscutting	To educate workforces about the meaning of innovation in the context the organiza-tion`s business model and each of the functional units and business units
Educate workforces about the organiza-tion's different dimensions of innovation	#2		Crosscutting	[Objectives related to each of the other innovation engagement programs or activities would be formulated]
Educate workforces about the significance of innovation	#1		Crosscutting	

Educate workforces about innovation and realizing organiza-tional vision	#2		Crosscutting	
Educate workforces about their potential to generate innovative ideas	#1		Crosscutting	
Educate workforces about the relationship between innovation and organiza-tional growth	#1		Crosscutting	
Educate workforces about innovation and career growth	#1		Crosscutting	

Publicize the Innovation-Support Program-Priority Listing

Once the innovation-support program priority listing tables are created, the next task is to distribute the final copies (hard and soft versions) to all workforces and leaders across functional units, along with a note that the next step of the process will be the HR innovation-support implementation plan.

Chapter 4

PHASE 3: IMPLEMENTATION

Overview

In order to fully engage in the material presented in this chapter, we must first review what has been covered so far. Remember, the HR innovation-support strategy model covered in this book is separated into four phases:

1. Analysis
2. Identification and prioritization of innovation-support programs
3. Implementation
4. Evaluation

This chapter discusses Phase Three of the HR innovation-support strategy, which is *implementation*.

Definition of Implementation

The Oxford Dictionary defines *implementation* as: a process of putting a decision or plan into effect or execution. In a technical sense, the word implementation is referred to within the context of the field or subject in which it is being applied. For instance, there is implementation in a scientific sense, implementation in engineering, implementation in computing, implementation in finance, implementation in insurance, and so on. So, what does the word *implementation* entail in the context of the HR innovation-support strategy model? In Chapter One, we defined the strategy as *a step by step process expressed or outlined in detailed statements of how various innovation-related tools, approaches, and actions that can be applied by HR to implement initiatives aimed at advancing workforce innovation across functional units to achieve an innovation-led organization.*

Therefore, *HR innovation-support strategy implementation* can be defined in this context as: a process that involves executing the innovation-support programs and activities listed on the priority-list into actual actions in order to accomplish the goals and purposes of the innovation-support strategy.

Importance of the HR Innovation-Support Implementation

As in any other type or context of strategy management (corporate, economic, social, etc.), implementation is the key determinant of the success of a strategy process. No matter how great or good an idea, plan, strategy, or policy is, it will amount to nothing if it is never implemented. In other words, creating statements that express intended innovation-support actions is meaningless to advancing innovation if the expressed statements of intent are not translated into *actions*.

An often-quoted *Fortune* magazine study found that 70% of the CEOs failures came not as a result of poor strategy formulation, but the inability to execute. This underscores the importance of the implementation phase in this book because this is the phase or process that moves the several statements of intent into actions that help create climate for workforce innovation.

In this chapter

We focus on the three important steps to take when creating the innovation-support strategy implementation (I-SSI) process. The first step is to create the *implementation plan*. This chapter focuses on the following steps:

- Step 1: Appointment of HR team and sub-committees to write the innovation-support strategy implementation plan
- Step 2: Preliminary aspects to consider
- Step 3: Content and format for the innovation-support strategy implementation plan

Step 1: Appointment of HR Committee

This step involves the following tasks:

- Head of HR should create a team—kind of ad-hoc—that will be responsible for drafting the innovation-support implementation plan. The teams should be allowed to create subcommittees.
- Head of HR should provide guidance on the roles, composition, and responsibilities. This will enable the committee to function efficiently and effectively.
- Head of HR should state time frame within which the draft and final HR innovation-support strategy implementation plan will be completed.

Note:

- Size, structure, composition, roles and responsibilities of the committee will depend on structural variables of the company such as the size, business model, and geographical context.
- Organizations with an established HR unit that focuses on driving the culture of innovation, would be responsible for developing and implementing the HR innovation-support strategy including drafting the innovation-support implementation plan.

Step 2: Preliminary Aspects to Consider

Once the committee(s) are constituted, here are some of the issues to consider.

- Appoint chairperson of the committee.
- Distribute writing roles i.e. allocating what section each member of the committee will write.
- Depending on the size of the innovation-support strategy implementation plan committee, sub-committees could be created for this purpose.
- Create an action plan for the overall task of writing the innovation-support strategy implementation plan.
- Write out how the evaluation and monitoring of the implementation plan will be done.

Step 3: Content and Format for the Innovation-Support Strategy Implementation Plan

The purpose of the HR innovation-support strategy implementation plan (I-SSIP) is to guide the organization on the activities of the innovation-support programs that will be championed and implemented across the organization over a specific period of time. Remember, the innovation support programs are aimed at two things: (1) help the organization meet or exceed its innovation goals across all functional units and (2) contribute to making innovation a collective function to all workforces.

Therefore, the I-SSIP should be written in a concise, simple, and well-ordered format to fulfil the intended communication to all stakeholders across the organization and execution of the programs and activities.

Illustration

For purposes of illustration, the following is a partial list of some brainstormed elements that would be included in the I-SSIP.

- Preface or introduction by the CEO
- Executive summary
- Innovation is every employee's responsibility
- HR innovation purpose
- Current innovation landscape of the organization
- Description of types of innovation-support programs
- Worksheets outlining the implementation of the innovation-support programs and activities

1. Preface or Introduction by the CEO

This section should have sentiments from the CEO. Here are some points that should be highlighted:

- The CEO's emotional interest and passion for innovation
- Articulate the following:
  - The innovation image of the company
  - How innovation is a key component of the company's corporate strategy. In other words, why innovation is a strategic priority to the company
  - How innovation is key to realizing the company vision
  - Why innovation is critical to sustainable competitiveness, resilience and growth
  - Why it is vital for every employee to be involved in advancing innovation
  - Why HR's role in advancing workforce innovation is critical

    o   Articulate the CEO and top leadership's commitment and support to ensuring that intended consequences of the HR innovation-support strategy are realized

2. Executive Summary

The executive summary innovation-support implementation plan (I-SSIP) should highlight the purpose and goal in relation to the innovation aspirations of functional units and the entire organization, thus, the statements being clear and concise. The statements should reference how innovation is being leveraged to realize the vision and mission of the company. Much of the information in this section should focus on the objectives of the HR innovation-support strategy. Doing so by referencing to the three categories of the innovation-support program, namely, innovation management programs, innovative thinking programs and innovation engagement programs. And that the programs will be implemented according to the innovation-support program priority listing. The section should allude to the objectives of the HR innovation-support strategy in terms of *meeting* or *exceeding* the organizational innovation goals that have been set across the functional units of the company, such as: (1) innovation ideas to be generated, (2) innovations to be launched or implemented, (3) revenues to be generated, and (4) cost savings gained from innovations launched or implemented within the time frame that was set. Above all, the section should make mention of the overall intended purpose of the HR innovation-support strategy in relation to driving the culture of innovation, innovation-led growth, and competitiveness in the company.

3. Innovation is Every Employee's Responsibility

Building on the sentiments of the executive summary, this section in your template should highlight:

- Why everyone in the organization should be involved in advancing innovation and how innovation relates to professional and career success of the workforces.
- Internal and external factors driving innovation in the organization.

4. Innovation Landscape of the Company

Remember, the main purpose of the HR innovation-support strategy is to drive, improve, or scale innovation performance of the company within a specified period of time. Against this backdrop, it is important to have a section that highlights the current innovation status of the company. So, this section would include the current status of the following aspects prior to the adoption of the HR innovation-support strategy:

- Number of radical and incremental innovation ideas generated.
- Number of patents obtained over a given period.
- Number of radical and incremental innovations launched over a given period.
- The company's existing innovation policies, practices and systems.
- A statement on how the HR innovation-support strategy under consideration intends to improve on the company's current innovation performance landscape.

You could state the anticipated improvement of innovation performance in terms of increasing the number of innovation ideas across functional units by a certain percentage, and also increase the revenue generated and cost-savings gained from innovations as a result of the HR innovation-support strategy.

5. Description of Categories of Innovation-Support Programs

Recall, at the beginning of Chapter Three this book has suggested three categories of innovation-support programs that are essential for developing and implementing an HR innovation-support strategy suggested. So, this section should describe what each of the categories of innovation-support programs entails, i.e.

- Category A: Innovation management programs
- Category C: Innovative thinking programs
- Category B: Innovation engagement programs

The description should highlight how the above categories of innovation-support are aimed at creating climate for advancing employee-driven innovation.

6. Creating Innovation-Support Strategy Implementation Plans

Let's look at the generic perspective. At a personal level, we have all undertaken projects before. Could be a house improvement project or a family camping trip. Take a camping trip, for example. There's a lot of action planning and preparation that takes place before a trip is undertaken. And during the trip, you implement some new tasks along the way with some necessary changes here and there. When you get to your destination, you ensure that all the planned activities are undertaken so that the trip is as memorable as planned or envisioned. The above analogy is a loose illustration of what an HR innovation-support strategy implementation plan entails. Back to the context of HR innovation-support strategy implementation plan, as said earlier, the HR innovation-support strategy implementation plan is a process that involves creating *action plans* to execute various innovation-related programs and activities in each of the innovation-support priority listing. In a nutshell, the HR innovation-support strategy implementation plan involves:

- Converting the categories of the HR innovation-support strategy into an actionable time-bound program with activities (i.e., three or six-month action plans).

- Translating the innovation-support programs into specifics that are implemented in a coordinated and effective manner.

- Creating a supporting budget that outlines how much it will cost (in terms of money) to implement activities in each of the categories of the innovation-support programs. The above aspects are then illustrated in a simple detailed action plan for execution. We have suggested two steps for executing the implementation plan.

Step One

Create an implementation plan for each of the three categories of the innovation-support programs (i.e., innovation management, innovative thinking, and innovation engagement), earmarked for execution within the timeframe of the HR innovation-support strategy; this could be two or three years.

Tables 4-1, 4-2, and 4-3 below are examples of templates for creating an HR innovation -support strategy implementation plan (I-SSIP).

Step Two

Create action plans for each program stipulated in the three categories of innovation-support programs.

Here is a list of some of the aspects that should be included in an innovation-support implementation plan and action plans for each program.

- Program and tasks /activities to be implemented
- Objectives for each program
- *When:* Implementation date of the task or program
- *How:* Decide whether the program will be outsourced or undertaken using internal expertise
- *Who:* The person(s)/committee or vendor responsible for undertaking the task or program
- *Order of priority:* Order by which the innovation-support programs or activities will be undertaken
- *Scale of the program:* Whether the program is functional unit specific or crosscutting; if functional unit specific, name the department.
- *Time frame:* Duration for undertaking the program
- *Resources:* Capabilities required to undertake the program or task
- *Outcome:* Expected outcome(s) of the program
- *Cost:* Financial resources required to adopt the program

Table 4-1. Innovation management programs implementation plan for 2 years (2020 - 2022)

Category of innovation-support program: *Innovation management*						
Overall objective of the programs: *To implement innovation management programs that are considered high priority across the organization*						
Date: February 3, 2020						
List of innovation management programs to be implemented	**Order of priority**	**Scale of the program**		**Time frame**	**Objective**	**Resources**
		Limited to Specific functional unit	**Crosscutting (to be implemented in all functional units)**			
Identifying and creating innovation priority areas (IPAs)	1		Crosscutting	2 months (February-March 2020)	To identify innovation priority areas across all functional units and business / product segments	(1) HR staff to collaborate with cross-functional units to create and implement IPAs (2) Create soft and hard copy publications of IPAs to be distributed to all workforces

Expected cost of the programs: The total amount of money required (if any) to undertake all the earmarked programs and activities of the action
Programs and activities review dates: For conducting reviews for all the programs and activities undergoing operation
Expected outcome: Implementation of all the earmarked innovation management programs and activities as stipulated

Since this is an illustration, the other innovation management programs listed below would be included in the table.

- Creating innovation priority areas
- Interpreting and creating dimensions of innovation
- Translating the meaning of innovation in the context of:
  - Formulating organizational innovation goals
  - Creating innovation roles
  - Creating innovation-challenge questions
- Innovation-idea management system
- Creating a mechanism for identifying and hiring innovation talent
- Creating a framework for innovation talent succession planning

- Creating a framework for measuring and reporting innovation performance

Table 4-2. Innovative thinking programs implementation plan for two years (2020 - 2022)

Category of innovation-support program: Innovative thinking						
Overall objective of the programs: *To implement programs that are considered high priority aimed at helping workforces develop innovative thinking abilities*						
Date: February 17, 2020						
List of innovative thinking programs to be implemented	Order of priority	Scale of the program		Time frame	Objective	Resources
		Limited to Specific functional unit	Crosscutting (implemented in all factional units)			
Questioning attribute	1		Crosscutting	1 month (February 2020)	To implement a range of programs and initiatives aimed at helping workforces develop questioning attributes	HR to create and implement a range of questioning-related programs

Expected cost of the programs: The total amount of money required (if any) to undertake all the earmarked programs and activities of the action

Programs and activities review dates: For conducting reviews for all the programs and activities undergoing operation

Expected outcome: Implementation of all the earmarked innovative thinking programs and activities as stipulated

Likewise, the other innovative thinking programs listed below would be included in the table.

- Associating attribute
- Experimenting attribute
- Networking attribute
- Envisioning attribute
- No fear-for-failure attribute
- Risk-taking attribute
- Challenging-status-quo attribute
- Grit attribute
- Thinking time attribute
- Educating managers about the importance of role-modelling in leading a culture of innovation

Table 4-3. Innovation engagement programs implementation plan for two years (2020 - 2022)

Category of innovation-support program: Innovation engagement						
Part 1 **Informative style** Programs aimed at educating workforces about the company`s innovation strategies, practices, policies and procedures						
Overall objective of the programs: *To implement programs for educating workforces about the company's innovation strategies, practices, policies and procedures*						
Date: February 4, 2020						
List of innovation engagement programs to be publicized	**Order of priority**	**Scale of the program**		**Time frame**	**Objective**	**Resources**
		Limited to Specific functional unit	**Crosscutting (implemented in all factional units)**			
Publicize and educate workforces about the following innovation management programs implemented by the organization: • Innovation priority areas • Interpreting and creating dimensions of innovation • Translating the meaning of innovation • Formulating organizational innovation goals • Creating innovation roles • Creating innovation-challenge questions • Innovation-idea management system • Identifying and hiring innovation talent	1		Crosscutting	6 months (February - June 2020)	To publicize and educate workforces about a range of innovation management programs implemented by the organization	HR staff to create and implement the publicity and educational materials

• Measuring and reporting innovation performance						

Expected cost of the programs: The total amount of money required (if any) to undertake all the earmarked programs and activities of the action

Programs and activities review dates: For conducting reviews for all the programs and activities undergoing operation

Expected outcome: Implementation of all the earmarked innovative thinking programs and activities as stipulated

Part 2
Inspirational style
The use of innovation-motivating slogans, catchphrases, and visual illustrations to educate workforces about various aspects of innovation

Overall objective of the programs: *To educate workforces by the use of innovation-motivating slogans, catchphrases, and visual illustrations to educate workforces about various aspects of innovation listed in this table*

Date: February 4, 2020

List of innovation engagement programs to be implemented	Order of priority	Scale of the program		Time frame	Objective	Resources
		Limited to Specific functional unit	**Cross-cutting** *(implemented in all functional units)*			
Educate workforces about the: • Meaning of innovation in the contexts of the organization's different functional activities • Dimensions of innovation in the context of the organization's functional activities • Significance of innovation	#1			6 months (February – June 2020)	To educate workforces by the use of innovation-motivating slogans, catchphrases, and visual illustrations about various aspects of innovation listed in this table	HR • External vendors

• Link between innovation and realizing organizational vision • Potential that workforces possess to generate innovative ideas • The relationship between innovation and organizational growth • Link between innovation and career growth of workforces						

Expected cost of the programs: The total amount of money required (if any) to undertake all the earmarked programs and activities of the action

Programs and activities review dates: For conducting reviews for all the programs and activities undergoing operation

Expected outcome: Implementation of all the earmarked innovation engagement programs and activities as stipulated

Action Plans

When creating innovation-support strategy implementation plans, two steps are suggested: (1) create HR innovation-support strategy implementation plan, and (2) create the individual action plans for each of the innovation-support programs listed in the implementation plan.

An *action plan* is comprised of a sequence of specific tasks or activities (adopted from the HR innovation-support strategy implementation plan) listed in the form of a template that should be performed or undertaken for the HR innovation-support strategy to succeed. That being said, each or most of the innovation-support programs listed in the implementation plan should be outlined in an action plan and performed to achieve the goals of the HR innovation-support strategy. Important aspects to be included in an *action plan*:

- *Category of innovation-support program*: Specify the category of innovation-support program (i.e. innovation management, innovative thinking or innovation engagement)
- *Program and tasks /activities*: To be undertaken
- *Objectives for each program*: What program or activity seeks to achieve
- *When:* Date for beginning the implementation of the task or program
- *How:* Will it be outsourced or conducted by internal expertise?
- *Who:* The person(s)/committee/ or vendor responsible for undertaking the task or program
- *Order of priority:* Order by which the innovation-support programs or activities will be undertaken.
- *Scale of the program:* Whether the program is limited to specific functional units or crosscutting
- *Time frame:* Duration for undertaking the program
- *Resources:* Capabilities required to undertake the program or task
- *Outcome:* Expected outcome of the program
- *Cost:* Financial resources required to undertake the program
- *Review of activities:* Conducting reviews for all the programs and activities undergoing implementation

Action Plan Template

Here is an example of a template with spaces for each of the aspects listed above.

Table 4-4. Example of an action plan template

Category of innovation-support program:								
Overall purpose of the program(s)								
Date:								
Name of programs or activities	When	Objective	Order of priority	Scale of the program	How	Who	Time frame	Resources

Expected cost of the programs: Total amount of money required to undertake all the programs and activities outlined in the action plan

Review dates: For conducting reviews for all the programs and activities outlined in the action plan undergoing implementation

Expected outcome: Complete implementation of all programs and activities outlined in the action plan

Chapter 5

PHASE 4: EVALUATION

Overview

Remember, HR innovation-support strategy entails written expressions describing a process that involves identifying and applying the right innovation-related tools and activities across functional units to create an environment in which every employee is encouraged, motivated, and enabled to take part in advancing innovation. By doing so, a culture of innovation is created in which innovation is every employee's job.

Question is, how does the definition or description fit into the practical sense of an organization? In answering this question, we return to our fictitious company, Walu Technologies, which has the following functional units:

Core units

- Product development division, comprising the following units:
  - Software segment
  - Cloud storage segment
  - Cybersecurity segment
- Marketing department, comprising the following units:
  - Product pricing

- ○ Product delivery process
- ○ Product promotion
- ○ New markets
- Customer service department

Support units

- Procurement department
- HR department
- Finance and accounting department
- IT department

As earlier stated, systemizing innovation using the HR innovation-support strategy would entail developing and implementing innovation-oriented programs in the context of each of the eight functional units of Walu Technologies. The evaluation phase ensures that the innovation-support programs and activities implemented are effective in producing the intended innovation performance consequences in terms of meeting or exceeding the innovation goals.

Remember, the HR innovation-support strategy suggested in this book is segmented into five phases: *analysis, identification and prioritization of programs, implementation*, and *evaluation*. We have so far discussed phases one, two, and three. As important all the three phases are to the process of HR innovation-support strategy, the exercise would be rendered less meaningful without an effective mechanism to examine and determine whether the goals and purpose of the HR innovation-support strategy have been realized.

In the preceding sections of this book, we have repeatedly defined what this model of the HR innovation-support strategy entails. In simple terms, it entails identifying, developing, and implementing a range of innovation-support programs and activities aimed at advancing innovation across functional units of an organization on a continual basis. In essence, what we have covered in the three chapters or three phases of the HR innovation-support strategy is a *means* to an *end*. This chapter (evaluation) answers the question, *how do you examine and determine the effectiveness of phases one, two and three?* In other words, since the purpose of the HR innovation-support strategy is to create and sustain a culture of innovation or innovation performance, then the *evaluation phase* examines and determines its effectiveness. Since the evaluation phase is one of the most crucial stages of the HR innovation-support strategy, it (the evaluation) must possess an effective mechanism to determine the efficacy of the innovation-support programs and activities implemented.

The evaluation phase is divided into three aspects:

1. Monitoring the HR innovation-support strategy implementation plan
2. Measuring innovation performance
3. Structuring an evaluation report

In this chapter

We focus on the following:

- Definition of the Evaluation Model
- Three-step Evaluation Model
  - ○ Step 1: Monitoring implementation plan
  - ○ Step 2: Measuring innovation performance
  - ○ Step 3: Structuring an evaluation report
- Conclusion and improvements
- Summary

Definition of the Evaluation Model

We start with the definition of the word *evaluation*. According to the online dictionary, Merriam-Webster, evaluation means "determination or value of something".

Context of Evaluating HR Innovation-Support Strategy

This book defines evaluation of HR innovation-support strategy as: a process that involves eliciting data from all the innovation-support programs implemented over a specified period and determining value created in terms of innovation performance across all the functional units of the company.

Three-Step Evaluation Model

This book has adopted an evaluation model with three steps:

- Step 1: Monitoring implementation plan
- Step 2: Measuring innovation performance
- Step 3: Structuring an evaluation report

Step 1: Monitoring Implementation Plan

This monitoring segment is against the backdrop of the HR innovation-support strategy implementation and action plans being embedded with a review requirement. Therefore, the monitoring implementation plan is aimed at fulfilling that purpose. Remember, the timeframe for HR innovation-support strategy can range anywhere from two to three years. This means that depending on the timeframe, it is important to embed regular incremental reviews aimed at ensuring that implementation of the innovation-support programs and activities is on course and, to make necessary corrective changes and improvements as the HR innovation-support strategy is under implementation via action plans.

Monitoring implementation of the innovation-support programs involves systematic collection of information on a regular basis from innovation-support programs undergoing implementation via action plans and use the information to check progress against the action plans of various programs and activities.

When does the monitoring process begin? Assuming the HR innovation-support strategy timeframe is two years, the process could be embedded with quarterly reviews that fit the timeframe (i.e. every 3 months), and then conduct a year-end main evaluation report of the HR innovation-support strategy. Depending on how the HR innovation-support strategy implementation plan is managed, assuming each of the three categories of innovation-support programs; *innovation management, innovative thinking,* and *innovation engagement* is being implemented by separate teams, each team should conduct and produce their monitoring reviews.

Indicators to be Monitored

There are several aspects and indicators that can be used as basis for conducting review analysis of the HR innovation-support strategy implementation process. We suggest that you use indicators that the team will easily understand and be able to relate them to the aspects being assessed.

Usually, there is a temptation to use many unnecessary indicators, which should be avoided. This book has suggested four indicators, namely: time frame, money, quality, and effectiveness.

Time frame: Are the programs or tasks on course to be implemented within the time frame stated in the action plan?

Money: If there is money allocated for implementation of the programs or tasks, are the activities within budget?

Quality: Is the implementation progress of the programs or tasks satisfactory in line with the expected outcome?

Effectiveness: Are there initial signs of achieving the intended consequences of the of programs or tasks that have been implemented so far?

Action Plan Review Template

The indicators highlighted would be used in the sample of a template below for reviewing the HR innovation-support strategy implementation process.

Table 5-5. Example of action plan review template

Category of innovation-support program:				
Date:				
Innovation-support program(s) being reviewed	Time frame	Money	Quality	Effectiveness
Next review date:				

Step 2: Measuring Innovation Performance

The second step when evaluating the HR innovation-support strategy is to understand how to measure innovation performance, which is a vital aspect in the evaluation process. We have so far described the process of *reviewing* and *assessing* various innovation performance–related activities at the functional-unit and corporate levels of an organization. The data from this process is used as a basis for determining (through evaluation) the extent to which the goals of the various innovation programs and activities have been achieved.

Importance

Measuring innovation performance is a vital component of evaluating the HR innovation-support strategy. This is due to the following reasons:

- First, the number of metrics used to measure innovation performance will also be used to evaluate the efficacy of the HR innovation-support strategy.
- Second, the data generated is useful for determining the innovation-performance status of the organization in terms of whether the innovation goals, objectives, and targets that were set by various functional units and by the organization as a whole have been achieved. This data is vital for evaluating the HR innovation-support strategy.
- Third, data generated from the cross-functional innovation-performance reporting will be used in the evaluation report to examine and determine whether the organization's efforts in investing in innovation activities across functional units are yielding results.
- Fourth, the information generated from the innovation performance data is useful for suggesting recommendations and improvements in the evaluation report, especially going forward regarding the kind of innovation strategies that should be developed and implemented.

Metrics for Measuring Innovation Performance

This book suggests four metrics of innovation-performance measurement:

- Innovation input measurement
- Innovation output measurement
- Innovation results measurement
- Innovation impact measurement

Details of each of the above metrics as follows.

Innovation Input Measurement

This metric focuses on programs and interventions invested into the HR innovation-support strategy. So, measuring innovation input involves assessing all three categories of innovation-support programs implemented: *innovation management programs, innovative thinking programs,* and *innovation engagement programs* during the period under review.

Illustration

This section illustrates how to measure innovation inputs. Assuming we are measuring innovation inputs of innovation-support programs implemented over a particular period of time in the core and support functional units of Walu Technologies, there are two things that must be done:

1.   List the core and support functional units
2.   Create sample tables or templates for each of the three categories of the innovation support programs implemented during the period under review.

Core and Support Functional Units

Core units

- Product development division
  - ○   Software segment
  - ○   Cloud storage segment
  - ○   Cybersecurity segment

- Marketing department
  - ○ Product pricing
  - ○ Product delivery process
  - ○ Product promotion
  - ○ New markets
- Customer service department

Support units

- Procurement department
- HR department
- Finance and accounting department
- IT department

Templates

Tables 5-6, 5-7, and 5-8 are examples of templates that could be used to assess each of the three categories of the innovation support programs implemented in all the functional units of Walu Technologies during the period under review. The categories highlighted in the three tables are:

- Category A: Implementation measurement of innovation management programs
- Category B: Implementation measurement of innovative thinking programs
- Category C: Implementation measurement of innovation engagement programs

Table 5-6. Implementation measurement of innovation management programs

Category of innovation-support program: Innovation management					
Time frame under review: February – December, 2020					
Date: December 14, 2020					
List of innovation management programs under review	Order of priority	Scale of the program		Objective of the program	Outcome
		Limited to Specific functional unit	Crosscutting (to be implemented in all functional units)		
Innovation priority areas (IPAs)				To ensure that each functional unit understood their innovation priority areas	Visually illustrated map showing company-wide priority areas to focus innovation
Interpreting and creating dimensions of innovation				• To ensure that each employee understood types of innovation in the context of their functional activities • To ensure that each employee understood how the concept of innovation degree (radical/incremental) relates to all the types of innovation identified	• Identified and created types of innovation for each functional unit of Walu Technologies • Visually illustrated booklet showing the company's context of types of innovation • Adoption of the types of innovation by each functional unit

				and adopted by each functional unit	• Visual illustration of description and application of the concept of innovation degree (radical and incremental) in included in the booklet
Translating the meaning of innovation				• To ensure that each employee understood the meaning of innovation in the context of their functional activities • To ensure that employees are able to generate innovative ideas in the context of their functional activities	• Developed and adopted definitions of innovation in each of the core and support functional units
Formulating organizational innovation goals				• To ensure that functional units understood to formulate innovation goals in the context of their	• Created a framework for formulating innovation goals

				functional activities • To ensure that each functional unit is able to formulate some innovation goals	• Trained all managers on how to formulate organizational innovation goals • Each functional unit has formulated some innovation goals
Creating innovation roles				• To ensure each functional unit includes some innovation roles in the job descriptions of the job positions	• Formulation and integration of innovation-performance job descriptions in 80% of the job positions across functional units of the company
Creating innovation-challenge questions				• To ensure that each functional unit formulates a list of innovation-challenge questions in the context of the functional activities	• Created a booklet with guidelines of how to formulate innovation-challenge in each of the company's functional units

					• Total of 50 innova-tion-chal-lenge questions formulated across all functional units
Innova-tion-idea management system				• To ensure that employees under-stand the innova-tion-idea man-agement guidelines designated for the generation and devel-opment of innova-tion-ideas in their functional units	• Visually illustrated booklet outlining compa-ny-wide innova-tion-idea man-agement guidelines • Adoption of the innova-tion-idea man-agement practices across functional units in the last 6 months
Identifying and hiring innovation talent				• To ensure that heads of depart-ments can identify and hire job candidates with the required mix of innovation skillsets for both	• Booklet outlin-ing the company's frame-work for identifying and hiring innovation talent

				experi- enced and entry level hires.	• Trained all managers on how to identify and hire innovation talent • Adoption of some innovation talent re- cruitment practices across functional units in the last 6 months
Measur- ing and reporting innovation performance				• To ensure that each functional unit can create and adopt a framework for meas- uring and reporting innovation perfor- mance of their functional units	• Visually illustrated booklet outlining styles for measuring, presenting, reporting innovation perfor- mance across functional units • Trained all managers on how to measure and report innovation perfor- mance

					• Adoption of reporting and presentation styles for innovation performance by 90% of the functional units

Table 5-7. Implementation measurement of innovative thinking programs

Category of innovation-support program: *Innovative thinking*					
Time frame under review: February – December, 2020					
Date: December 14, 2020					
List of innovative thinking-related programs under review	**Order of priority**	**Scale of the program**		**Objective of the program**	**Outcome**
		Limited to Specific functional unit	**Crosscutting** *(to be implemented in all functional units)*		
• Questioning attribute • Associating attribute • Experimenting attribute • Networking attribute • Envisioning attribute • No fear-of-failure attribute • Risk-taking attribute • Challenging-status-quo attribute • Grit attribute • Thinking time attribute				To ensure that employees across all functional units learn and understand how to develop most of the innovative thinking-related programs	Visually illustrated booklet outlining: • What each of the listed attributes entail and relate to developing an innovative thinking mindset. • Tools on how workforces can develop the listed attributes • An increase in the number of radical and incremental innovative ideas generated across functional units.

Table 5-8. Implementation measurement of innovation engagement programs

Category of innovation-support program: *Innovation engagement*					
Time frame under review: February – December, 2020					
Date: December 14, 2020					
Part 1 **Informative style**					
Programs aimed at educating workforces about the company's innovation strategies, practices, policies and procedures					
List of innovation engagement-related programs under review	**Order of priority**	**Scale of the program**		**Objective of the program**	**Outcome**
		Limited to Specific functional unit	**Crosscutting** *(to be implemented in all functional units)*		
Publicize and educate workforces about the following innovation management programs implemented by the organization: • Innovation priority areas • Interpreting and creating dimensions of innovation • Translating the meaning of innovation • Formulating organizational innovation goals • Creating innovation roles				To publicize and educate workforces about a range of innovation management programs and policies implemented by the organization	To create and implement the publicity and educational materials

• Creating innova-tion-chal-lenge questions • Innova-tion-idea management system • Identifying and hiring innovation talent • Measuring and reporting innovation performance					

Part 2
Inspirational style

The use of innovation-motivating slogans, catchphrases, and visual illustrations to educate workforces about various aspects of innovation

List of innovation engagement-re-lated programs under review	Order of priority	Scale of the program		Objective of the program	Outcome
		Limited to Specific functional unit	**Crosscutting** *(to be imple-mented in all functional units)*		
Educate work-forces about the: • Meaning of innovation in the context of each of the organ-ization's functional activities • Dimensions of innovation in the con-text of each organization-al functional activities • Significance of innovation				To educate workforc-es about various aspects of innova-tion such as listed in this table by use of innova-tion-mo-tivating slogans, catch-phrases,	• Creating and implementing channels for communicat-ing various innova-tion-motivat-ing slogans, catchphrases, and visual illustrations. Examples of communica-tion channels include:

• Link between innovation and realizing organizational vision • Potential that workforces possess and generate innovative ideas • Relationship between innovation and organizational growth • Link between innovation and career growth of workforces				and visual illustrations	○ Plaques inscribed with innovation-motivating slogans or catch-phrases ○ Innovation-motivating slogans on company uniforms ○ Monitors displaying innovation-motivating slogans ○ Innovation-motivating slogans on calendars ○ Innovation-motivating posters ○ Innovation-motivating slogans on pens ○ Other channels include mugs, bags, T-shirts etc.

						• Passion and emotional interest for innovation attitudes exhibited by many work-forces
						• Noticeable interest for engagement in innova-tion-related conversations by work-forces across functional units
						• A general increase in generation of ideas across functional units.

Innovation Output Measurement

This section looks at the second measurement, the *innovation output*. Before we dive into the details of measuring innovation output, it is important to understand what it entails. First, *innovation output measurement* is defined as: a type of metric that involves determining the number of innovation ideas generated by workforces across functional units as a consequence of the various initiatives (innovation inputs) implemented by the organization over a specified period of time.

In other words, innovation output includes *the number of innovation ideas generated in the context of the organization's functional units and business segments.* Innovation output is the first evidence to manifest as a consequence of the innovation inputs (i.e. innovation-support programs undertaken over a specific period)—that is why it is characterized as *innovation outputs* because the innovation ideas are a result of the specific innovation programs or interventions undertaken over a specified time period of the HR innovation-support strategy.

Two Perspectives

In this book, innovation output is divided into two perspectives: (1) the number of innovation ideas *generated* by workforces over a specified period and (2) the number of innovation ideas *undergoing* development.

Illustration

How do you determine innovation output of Walu Technologies? Two steps: First, outline the core and support functional units. Second, determine the innovation ideas generated and the innovation ideas undergoing development.

The core and support functional units of Walu Technologies are as follows:

Core units

- Product development division:
  - Software segment
  - Cloud storage segment
  - Cybersecurity segment
- Marketing department:
  - Product pricing
  - Product delivery process
  - Product promotion
  - New markets
- Customer service department

Support units

- Procurement department
- HR department
- Finance and accounting department
- IT department

Determine Innovation Ideas Generated and Undergoing Development

This section illustrates the number of innovation ideas generated and how many ideas are undergoing development across the core and support functional units of the company.

Tables 5-8 to 5-12 provide examples of innovation ideas generated and undergoing development in core and support functional units of the company during the period under review for the HR innovation-support strategy.

Table 5-9 provides the combined number of innovation ideas generated and ideas undergoing development for all the three product segments listed below. We could also create tables for each of the product segments, but for purposes of illustration we went for a combined option.

- Software solutions
- Cloud storage solutions
- Cybersecurity solutions

Table 5-9. Product innovation ideas generated and ideas undergoing development

Number of product innovation ideas generated and ideas undergoing development	
Time frame under review: February – December, 2020	
Date: December 17, 2020	
Radical and increment product innovation ideas generated	
Radical product innovation ideas	Incremental product innovation ideas
20	35
Radical and increment software-product innovation ideas undergoing development	
Radical product innovation ideas	Incremental product innovation ideas
10	15

Marketing units

- Product pricing
- Product delivery
- Product promotion
- New markets

Table 5-10. Product pricing innovation ideas generated and ideas undergoing development

Number of product pricing innovation ideas generated and ideas undergoing development	
Time frame under review: February – December, 2020	
Date: December 19, 2020	
Radical and incremental product-pacing innovation ideas generated	
Radical product pricing innovation ideas	Incremental product-pricing innovation ideas
9	15
Radical and incremental product-pricing innovation ideas undergoing development	
Radical product-pricing innovation ideas undergoing development	Incremental product-pricing innovation ideas undergoing development
3	7

Similar tables would be created for the following types of marketing innovation ideas generated.

- Product delivery innovation ideas
- Product promotion innovation ideas
- New markets

Table 5-11. Product pricing innovation ideas generated and ideas undergoing development

Number of product pricing innovation ideas generated and ideas undergoing development	
Time frame under review: February – December, 2020	
Date: December 19, 2020	
Radical and incremental product-pacing innovation ideas generated	
Radical product pricing innovation ideas	Incremental product-pricing innovation ideas
9	15
Radical and incremental product-pricing innovation ideas undergoing development	
Radical product-pricing innovation ideas undergoing development	Incremental product-pricing innovation ideas undergoing development
3	7

Similar tables would be created for the following types of marketing innovation idea generated:

- Product delivery innovation ideas
- Product promotion innovation ideas
- New markets

Customer service

Customer service innovations are usually designed to support the delivery of product offerings at different stages: *before purchase*, *during purchase*, and *after purchase*. Hence, the customer service innovation ideas generated could be presented according to the following categories:

- Customer service innovation ideas designed to support the delivery of product offerings *before* purchase
- Customer service innovation ideas designed to support the delivery of product offerings *during* purchase
- Customer service innovation ideas designed to support the delivery of product offerings *after* purchase
- Customer service innovation ideas aimed at improving the quality of interaction between the company and its customers at all touchpoints

Table 5-12 Illustrates the number of radical and incremental customer service innovation ideas generated during the period under review for the HR innovation-support strategy.

Table 5-12. Customer service innovation ideas generated and ideas undergoing development

Number of customer service innovation ideas generated and ideas undergoing development	
Time frame under review: February – December, 2020	
Date: December 19, 2020	
Radical and increment customer service innovation ideas	
Radical customer service innovation ideas	Incremental customer service innovation ideas
9	17
Before-purchase radical and increment customer service innovation ideas undergoing development	
Radical innovation ideas	Incremental innovation ideas
5	7

Support units

Usually, innovation ideas generated in support functional units are for *cost-saving* and *efficiency* purposes, such as:

- Procurement department
- HR department
- Finance and accounting department
- IT department

Table 5-13 the number of radical and incremental cost saving innovation ideas generated in the support functional units during the period under review for the HR innovation-support strategy.

Table 5-13. Cost-saving innovation ideas generated and ideas undergoing development for support functional units

Number of cost-saving innovation ideas generated and ideas undergoing development in support functional units	
Time frame under review: February – December, 2020	
Date: December 22, 2020	
Radical and incremental cost-saving innovation ideas generated	
Radical innovation ideas	Incremental innovation ideas
10	12
Cost-saving innovation ideas undergoing development	
Radical innovation ideas	Incremental innovation ideas
7	9

You would also create individual tables for the number of innovation ideas generated for each of the support functional unit (in parentheses):

- Procurement department (*cost-saving procurement innovation ideas*)
- HR department (*cost-saving HR innovation ideas*)
- Finance and accounting department (*cost-saving accounting innovation ideas*)
- IT department (*cost-saving IT innovation ideas*)

Innovation-Results Measurement

So far, we have looked at two metrics of measuring innovation performance: innovation input measurement and innovation output measurement. The third metric of measuring innovation performance is *innovation-results measurement.*

Definitions

To understand innovation-results measurement, it is first necessary to fully understand the meaning of the term. According to the *Merriam-Webster* online dictionary, the word *result* means "a final consequence of a sequence of actions or events expressed qualitatively or quantitatively."

In the context of innovation, the interpretation of *innovation results* is a series of consequences of innovation management–related actions and activities. Recall that Chapter Three, highlighted innovation-idea management systems as one of the critical aspects in implementing a successful HR innovation-support strategy. We illustrated how innovation ideas go through an assessment process that leads to the conversion of the innovation ideas into innovations. The point is that an innovation is essentially the end product or end result of an innovation idea that has proceeded through a rigorous development process. Then, what does the term *innovation results* mean?

Definition of Innovation Results

This book's definition of *innovation results* is based on two things: first, innovations are an end product of innovation ideas, and second, the basic meaning of the word *results* is "a final consequence of a sequence of actions and activities." Thus, this book defines *innovation results* as a resultant end product of the innovation-idea assessment and development processes in the context of a particular type of innovation and innovation degree.

Definition of Innovation-Results Measurement

This book defines *innovation-results measurement* as a process that involves determining whether the intended final resultant end product of the development or conversion process of an innovation idea was realized.

Illustration

As in previous sections, this section uses the functional units of Walu Technologies to illustrate the number of innovations launched or implemented during the period under review for HR innovation-support strategy.

Product-development department

Table 5-14 outlines the combined number of radical and incremental product innovations launched in the product-development by the three product segments listed below during the period under review:

- Software solutions
- Cloud storage solutions
- Cybersecurity solutions

Table 5-14. Product innovations launched

Number of product innovations launched	
Time frame under review: February – December, 2020	
Date: December 18, 2020	
Number of radical and increment product innovations launched	
Radical product innovations	Incremental product innovations
5	10

Marketing units

- Product pricing
- Product delivery
- Product promotion
- New markets

Table 5-15 shows an example of the number of marketing innovations launched during the period under review.

Table 5-15. Product-pricing innovations launched

Number of product-pricing innovations launched	
Time frame under review: February – December, 2020	
Date: December 20, 2020	
Radical and increment product-pricing innovations launched	
Radical product-pricing innovations launched	Incremental product-pricing innovations launched
3	7

Similar tables would be created for the following other types of marketing innovations.

- Product delivery innovations
- Product promotion innovations

Absent from this list is the new-markets unit; because of the different format used for presenting the results of this unit, it is covered separately in the following subsection.

Characterization of Innovation in the Context of New Markets

Note that the context of interpreting or expressing the extent of the newness or novelty of an innovation for new markets is different from the contexts of other types of marketing innovations, such as innovations in product packaging, pricing, product promotion and product delivery.

When it comes to presenting innovations about new markets discovered, the phrases *new unserved market* and *new-market segment* are used to characterize the extent of newness or novelty of the new-market ideas generated. *New-market innovations* refers to discovering novel markets not served by the organization or its competitors for existing products and services. In this book, new markets are categorized in the contexts of *new unserved markets* and *new-market segments*, defined as follows:

- *New unserved markets*: This involves discovering customer audiences for the company's existing products and services in a *completely new geographical location* unserved by the company or its competitors.
- *New-market segments*: This involves discovering *new customer segments* for the company's *existing products and services* within an *already-served geographical location*. In other words, it involves the discovery of new-market segments in a larger geographical location already served by

both the company and its competitors. This can be thought of as an "incremental" new-market discovery.

Table 5-16 shows the context of the number of new markets.

Table 5-16. New markets discovered

Number of new markets discovered	
Time frame under review: February – December, 2020	
Date: December 20, 2020	
New-unserved markets and new-market segments	
New-unserved markets	New-market segments
5	8

Customer service

Table 5-17 shows an example of an outline of number of radical and incremental customer service (*before-purchase, during-purchase and after-purchase*) innovations launched or implemented during the period under review for the HR innovation-support strategy.

Table 5-17. Customer service innovations launched or implemented

Number of customer service innovations launched or implemented	
Time frame under review: February – December, 2020	
Date: December 20, 2020	
Radical and increment customer service innovations launched or implemented	
Number of radical customer service innovations	Number of incremental customer service innovations
3	5

Support units

The innovations in support functional units (as listed) are usually for *cost-saving* and *efficiency* purposes:

- Procurement department
- HR department
- Finance and accounting department
- IT department

Table 5-18 illustrates the overall number of radical and incremental innovations implemented in the above support functional units during the period under review.

Table 5-18. Cost-saving innovations implemented

Number of cost-saving innovations implemented in support functional units	
Time frame under review: February – December, 2020	
Date: December 22, 2020	
Number of radical and increment cost-saving innovations implemented in support functional units	
Radical cost-saving innovations	Incremental cost-saving innovations
5	7

You could also create individual tables for innovations implemented by each of the support functional unit (in parentheses):

- Procurement department (*cost-saving procurement innovations*)
- HR department (*cost-saving HR innovations*)

- Finance and accounting department (*cost-saving accounting innovations*)
- IT department (*cost-saving IT innovations*)

Innovation Impact Measurement

With a clear understanding of three metrics for measuring innovation performance (innovation input measurement, innovation output measurement, and innovation-results measurement), we are ready for the last metric: *innovation impact measurement.*

Definition of Innovation Impact Metric

According to the *Merriam-Webster* online dictionary, the word *impact* means "to have an effect on something". In the context of this book, *innovation impact* can be defined as an innovation-performance metric that captures the monetary effect of an innovation on the organization.

Definition of Innovation Impact Measurement

Innovation impact measurement can be defined as: *a metric of innovation-performance measurement that involves determining the effect of an innovation on the organization's commercial and monetary value in terms of revenue, cost savings, and other aspects, such as market share, stock price, and market value.*

Illustration

As in previous cases, we will use the functional units of Walu Technologies to illustrate the innovation impact measurement.

As stated earlier, the monetary value is expressed in terms of the *revenues* generated from radical and incremental innovations launched and the *cost savings* gained from radical and incremental cost-saving innovations implemented during the period under review for HR innovation-support strategy.

As in previous sections, we will use the tables to express the innovation impact measurement. Therefore, the example of *revenues* generated and *cost savings* gained are outlined in the tables 5-19, 5-20, 5-21, 5-22 and 5-23. We begin with the product-development department with the following product segments:

- Software solutions
- Cloud storage solutions
- Cybersecurity segment

Table 5-19. Revenue generated by product innovations launched by the above three product segments

Revenues generated by radical and incremental product innovations launched during under review	
Time frame under review: February – December, 2020	
Date: December 22, 2020	
Revenues generated by radical and incremental product innovations launched by the company`s three product segments: Software, cloud storage, and cybersecurity	
Revenues by radical product innovations	Revenues by incremental product innovations
$7M	$5M

Marketing units

- Product pricing
- Product delivery
- Product promotion
- New markets

Table 5-20 shows an example of an outline of revenue generated by product-pricing innovations launched during the period under review.

Table 5-20. Revenues generated by product-pricing innovations

Revenues generated by radical and incremental product-pricing innovations launched during period under review	
Time frame under review: February – December, 2020	
Date: December 20, 2020	
Revenues generated by radical and incremental product-pricing innovations	
Revenues by radical product-pricing innovations	Revenues by incremental product-pricing innovations
$2.7	$1.8

Similar tables would be created for the revenues generated by the other types of marketing innovations listed below.

- Product delivery innovations
- Product promotion innovations

New markets

As mentioned earlier, *new-market innovations* refer to discovering novel markets not served by the organization or its competitors for existing products and services. In this book, revenue generated by new markets is categorized by *new unserved markets* and *new-market segments*, as outlined in Table 5-21.

Table 5-21. Revenues generated by new markets

Revenues generated by new-unserved markets and new-market segments discovered during the period under review	
Time frame under review: February – December, 2020	
Date: December 20, 2020	
Revenues generated by new-unserved markets and new-market segments	
Revenues by new-unserved markets	Revenues by new-market segments
$2.7	$1.8

Support units

As mentioned earlier, innovations in support functional units are usually for *cost-saving* and *efficiency* purposes. This section outlines *cost-savings* gained from innovations implemented in support functional units.

- Procurement department
- HR department
- Finance and accounting department
- IT department

Table 5-22 shows an example of the savings gained from the number of radical and incremental cost-saving innovations implemented in the above support functional units during the period under review for the HR innovation-support strategy.

Table 5-22. Cost-savings gained from innovations implemented in support functional units

Number of cost-savings gained from radical and incremental innovations implemented by support functional units	
Time frame under review: February – December, 2020	
Date: December 22, 2020	
Cost-savings gained from radical and incremental innovations in support functional units	
Cost savings from radical innovations implemented in support functional units	Cost savings from incremental innovations implemented in support functional units
$2m	$1.5m

You could also create individual tables for cost savings gained from innovations launched by each of the support functional unit (in parentheses):

- Procurement department (*cost-saving procurement innovations*)
- HR department (*cost-saving HR innovations*)
- Finance and accounting department (*cost-saving accounting innovations*)
- IT department (*cost-saving IT innovations*)

Step 3: Structuring an Evaluation Report

Recall at the beginning of Chapter Five we stated that this book has adopted a three-step evaluation model:

- Step 1: Monitoring implementation plan
- Step 2: Measuring innovation performance
- Step 3: Structuring an evaluation report

We have so far discussed Steps One and Two. The final step is structuring an evaluation report.

Assuming it is one year into the HR innovation-support strategy implementation plan and after two monitoring reports, it is time for the prime movers of the implementation plan to conduct the first-year evaluation of the HR innovation-support strategy implementation plan. Remember, Lewis Carroll's poem at the beginning of the book, "The Hunting of the Snark"? It says, "If you don't know where you are going, any road will take you there." Now it's time to look at the path you took. We did relate this quote to the HR innovation-support strategy as the path for creating a culture of innovation. So, it's time for the head of HR and the HR unit involved in driving the culture of innovation through the implementation of the HR innovation-support strategy, to ask questions about whether the path that was selected for driving the culture of innovation across the organization is paying off. If it is, in what context is the payoff? This question will be answered in this section on structuring an evaluation report, whose focus is to examine and determine the effectiveness of the HR innovation-support strategy in realizing the goal of attaining the culture of innovation. This is where the structure and content of the evaluation report comes in.

Brainstorm Style and Content

Keep in mind that there are different styles of presenting evaluation reports, depending on the nature of the organization and subject for which the evaluation is being conducted. In the following sections, we will look at elements that should be included in the evaluation report for the HR innovation-support strategy.

Before you begin to work on your draft evaluation report, it is important to understand that the returns from all the investment made, in terms of time, money, and effort to develop and implement the programs selected for the HR innovation-support strategy over the period of one year will be defined and revealed within the evaluation report. What does this mean? It means that you must adopt an evaluation reporting style that will present and communicate content in a simple manner that can be understood by all or the majority of the workforce.

To kickstart the process of writing the evaluation report, the head of HR should lead the HR unit responsible for developing and implementing the HR innovation-support strategy into a series of brainstorming sessions for structure and content of the evaluation report. This process can be tricky in that there is a temptation to cloud the evaluation report with unnecessary stuff. To avoid this, it is important and helpful to, (1) stick with some of the metrics used in the monitoring process (2) agree beforehand the number of metrics you will work with (i.e. three to five), (3) align your metrics with the initial purpose, goals or objectives of the HR innovation-support strategy (4) write easy-to-understand metrics by all levels of workforces, and (5) conduct as many brainstorming sessions as possible to improve on the ideas suggested about structure and content.

There are many styles of evaluation reporting. Here is an example of some the things that should be included when writing an evaluation report on the HR innovation-support strategy.

1. Preface
2. Executive summary
3. Summary of innovation-support programs
4. Evaluation criteria
5. Presentation format and evaluative questions
6. Conclusion and improvements

1. Preface

In Chapter Four when discussing the implementation phase, we gave an example of a presentation style. The preface had sentiments by the CEO. The same approach would be adopted when writing your evaluation report. That being said, this section should highlight:

- The CEO`s reference to some of sentiments in the preface section of the implementation plan. So, a number of the aspects should be reiterated, such as:

  ○ Why and how innovation is a strategic priority to the company

  ○ How innovation is key to realizing the company's vision

  ○ Why innovation is critical to sustainable competitiveness and growth

  ○ Why it is vital for every employee to be involved in advancing innovation

- Thank the HR team for their commitment and hard work in developing and managing such a complex process as the HR innovation-support strategy.

- Thank the organizational leadership and all workforces for their response, support and contribution to the results achieved so far in the first year of the HR innovation-support strategy.

- Thank the workforces for the innovation ideas generated across functional units, with some of them resulting in innovations that are providing revenue and cost saving benefits to the company. You could give examples of such innovations.

- How the culture of innovation is contributing to building a market-responsive, customer centric, resilient, and competitive company.

2.   Executive Summary

The executive summary of the first-year evaluation report should highlight the following:

- *Why the organization instituted the HR innovation-support strategy.* Include data about the innovation performance of the company at the time of implementation, such as, in the last three to five years:

  - Number of radical and incremental innovation ideas generated

  - Number of patents obtained

  - Number of radical and incremental innovations

  - Revenue generated and cost-savings gained

  - The company's existing innovation policies, practices, and systems

- *The aim of the evaluation report.* Here, you would outline in brief bullet points what the aim is of the evaluation.

- *The purpose and goals of instituting the HR innovation-support strategy in relation to the innovation performance goals of functional units and the organization.* You would outline purpose statements and innovation goals that relate to the following:

  - Create a culture of innovation where every employee is involved in contributing to generating innovation ideas across functional units.

  - Help the organization *meet* or *exceed* its corporate innovation goals for the period between February to December 2020.

○ Help functional units *meet* or *exceed* their functional unit innovation goals between February to December 2020.

3. Summary of Innovation-Support Programs

This section should outline all the three categories of innovation-support programs. Each of the programs implemented must be presented in a concise and easy-to-read-style. Tables 5-23, 5-24 and 5-25 are examples of innovation-support programs implemented in each of the three categories, namely, innovation management program, innovative thinking programs, and innovation engagement programs.

Table 5-23. List of innovation management programs implemented

HR innovation-support strategy programs
List of innovation management programs implemented - February to December, 2020
• Creating innovation priority areas • Interpreting and creating dimensions of innovation • Translating the meaning of innovation in the context of each unit • Formulating organizational innovation goals • Creating innovation roles • Creating innovation-challenge questions • Innovation-idea management system • Creating a mechanism for identifying and hiring innovation talent • Creating a framework for innovation talent succession planning • Creating a framework for measuring and reporting innovation performance

Table 5-24. List of innovative thinking programs implemented

HR innovation-support strategy programs
List of innovative thinking programs implemented – February to December, 2020
• Questioning attribute • Associating attribute • Experimenting attribute • Networking attribute • Envisioning attribute • No fear-of-failure attribute • Risk-taking attribute • Challenging-status-quo attribute • Grit attribute • Thinking time attribute • Role-modeling in leading a culture of innovation

Table 5-25. List of innovation engagement programs implemented

HR innovation-support strategy programs
List of innovation engagement programs implemented February to December, 2020
Informative styles: **Publicity and workforce educational programs undertaken**
• Innovation priority areas • Interpreting and creating dimensions of innovation • Translating the meaning of innovation • Formulating organizational innovation goals • Creating innovation roles • Creating innovation-challenge questions • Innovation-idea management system • Identifying and hiring innovation talent • Measuring and reporting innovation performance

Inspirational styles: **motivating-slogans, catchphrases and visual illustrations created and publicized across the organization**
• Meaning of innovation in the context of the different functional activities • Dimensions of innovation in the context of the organization`s functional activities • Significance of innovation • Link between innovation and realizing organizational vision • Potential that workforces possess willingness to generate innovative ideas • The relationship between innovation and organizational growth • Link between innovation and career growth of workforces

4. Evaluation Criteria

When writing an evaluation report, this section should state criteria used to evaluate the HR innovation-support strategy. Before we dive into the evaluation criteria suggested for this book, it is important to mention a few things.

Evaluating the HR innovation support strategy is the final determination of the return on investment in innovation-support programs that have been implemented over the period under review. That being said, you want to use criteria that are easy to understand and effective in determining the assessment. There are two aspects that need to be understood about evaluation criteria. First and foremost, its meaning. According to an online business dictionary, the evaluation criteria are: *benchmark or yardstick comprising factors against which an accomplishment is measured.*

The second aspect is the type of evaluation criteria selected. In my experience with innovation projects, there is a tendency by organizations to apply evaluation criteria in a generic or mechanical manner, without regard to the context of the subject or intervention being examined, thus, impairing the relevance of the evaluation. Although it is a challenge in most cases of evaluation processes, it is important to come up with the evaluation criteria that mirror the context of the subject or intervention being evaluated, and it must be easy to understand.

The key to producing an accurate evaluative analysis is adopting relevant and easy-to-understand evaluation criteria. Simple here means that it must not lend itself to multiple interpretations. It is straightforward, formatted in an 'eye-pleasing' way, and gives pertinent information.

Creating evaluation criteria for an innovation strategy or innovation-support program can be tricky because of the manner of which innovation performance is generally measured. Earlier, when discussing innovation performance measurement (Step Two of this Chapter), stated the four perspectives of measuring innovation performance: *innovation input, innovation output, innovation-results,* and *innovation impact.*

In order to ensure that the evaluation is contextual and coherent with the purpose and goals of the HR innovation-support strategy, the evaluation criteria suggested is aligned with each of the (above) four listed metrics of measuring innovation.

Now it is time to outline each criterion that will be used to determine the evaluative conclusion. In line with the four metrics of measuring innovation, we have identified and suggested evaluation criteria comprising the following four factors:

- Relevance and efficiency of the innovation inputs
- Innovation ideation
- Innovation results
- Innovation impact

In the following sections, we will outline how each criterion should be described and presented in the HR innovation-support strategy evaluation report. In other words, the purpose of this section is to guide you on how to define and present each of the four-evaluation criterion when writing an evaluation report.

Relevance and Efficiency of Innovation-Inputs Criterion

In outlining what the criterion *relevance and efficiency of innovation inputs* entails, the first thing is to define the term *innovation inputs.* Here are a few examples of how it would be phrased:

- The term *innovation inputs* comprise of various innovation-support programs that have been implemented or invested into as part of the HR innovation-support strategy programs during the period under review.

- Second, the words *relevance* and *efficiency* are defined in the context of the term *innovation inputs:*

  o *Relevance* is the extent to which the objectives of each innovation-support program (innovation inputs) is consistent or in line with the innovation *needs* and *priorities* of the organization.
  o *Efficiency* involves assessing the extent to which the innovation-support programs were implemented within allocated resources (budget) and timeframe.

- Third, outline the importance of innovation inputs. For instance, you would say that creating a culture of innovation does not develop or happen naturally. Also, emphasize that you cannot create a culture of innovation across the organization using traditional, non-innovation-oriented management tools. Therefore, the implementation of innovation-support programs through the HR innovation-support strategy under review.

- Fourth, state the purpose of relevance and efficiency of the innovation inputs criterion. That it is meant to assess whether the innovation-support programs have been implemented according to the various action plans for implementing the HR innovation-support strategy.

Note to Reader: There are tables suggested later in this section that illustrate the relevance and efficiency of the innovation-inputs criterion (i.e. Tables 5-26, 5-27 and 5-28).

Innovation Ideation Criterion

Earlier in this chapter, when discussing the four metrics of measuring innovation performance in Step Two, *innovation output* was defined as a type of metric used to determine the number of radical and incremental ideas generated across functional units. Since innovation-idea generation is a key indicator of output of investment in innovation-support programs, this book has adopted *innovation ideation* as the second evaluation criterion.

So, when it comes to this section, here is an example of what would be outlined:

- Provide a statement outlining what innovation ideation criterion entails. For example, it is a performance measure for assessing innovation ideas generated because of the implementation of the HR innovation-support strategy during the period under review.

- Innovation idea generation is a source of any innovation, therefore, a vital indicator of success of the HR innovation-support strategy.

- Innovation ideation criterion has been applied to all the core and support functional units of the company, and that this is presented in the next section titled *innovation performance* and *evaluative questions*.

- The innovation ideation criterion has been applied to both radical and incremental innovation ideas generated during the period under review, (please, refer to the section of the report on *innovation performance* and *evaluative questions*).

Innovation Results Criterion

The third criterion is *innovation results*. Remember, in Step Two, when discussing innovation measurement, we defined *innovation results* as an end-product of the innovation-idea assessment and development processes in the context of a particular type of innovation and innovation degree. This book has adopted *innovation results* as the third evaluation criterion when assessing success of the HR innovation-support strategy for the period under review. There are examples of some of the things that should be outlined in this section:

- The purpose of the HR innovation-support strategy is to broaden the organization's definition and types of innovation; thus, this is a vital indicator of success.

- An organization cannot realize the mission of creating a culture of innovation without broadening the definition and types of innovation in the context of the organization's functional activities. So, the innovation results criterion assesses whether the organization's quest for broadening the definition and types of innovation is on course and in line with the goal of the HR innovation-support strategy.

- Innovations launched or implemented represent a huge indicator of success and contribution to the organization's culture of innovation.

- Over the period under review, the organization has invested a great deal of resources aimed at boosting and sustaining innovation capabilities of the organization. Therefore, innovations launched or implemented represent major indicator of the company's return on its investment in various innovation-support programs across the organization during the period under review.

- The innovation results criterion will be applied to all the core and support functional units, and that this is presented in the next section titled presentation format and evaluation.

- The innovation results criterion would also be applied to both radical and incremental innovations launched or implemented during the period under review.

- If deemed necessary, you may provide a note here, saying that the innovation results criterion is interpreted in the section titled; innovation performance and evaluative questions.

Innovation Impact Criterion

The fourth criterion is *innovation impact*. In Step Two, we defined *innovation impact* as "an innovation-performance measurement that involves determining the effect of an innovation on the organization's commercial and monetary value in terms of revenue, cost savings, and other aspects, such as market share, stock price, and market value". The overall goal of an HR innovation-support strategy is monetary contribution. So, it is important to include an evaluation criterion that specifically assesses and determines the monetary impact as the main success factor of the HR innovation-support strategy. That being said, here is an example of some of the aspects to include in this section:

- Provide a statement outlining *what innovation impact criterion* entails. For example, you would say that it is a performance measure for assessing the effectiveness of the company's HR innovation-support strategy that has been under implementation for a year.

- Explain why the innovation impact criterion is vital. For instance:

  o That, all three evaluation criteria discussed so far are important to providing guideposts for determining success of the HR innovation-support strategy. However, the *innovation impact* is a critical *criterion.*

○ That, the broad range of innovation-support programs implemented across the functional units of the organization during the period under review, has offered a great deal of enlightening perspectives of opportunities to the organization in terms of knowledge and experience. For instance, (1) understanding intricacies of what innovation entails, (2) undertaking the process of the HR innovation-support strategy much better in the next cycle, and (3) knowing the meaning of innovation capabilities and cross functional collaborations in relation to building an organization-wide culture of innovation.

○ You could also mention that the company has gained a lot of value from the entire process of the HR innovation-support strategy.

• That, one of the ultimate goals of the HR innovation-support strategy is to create and sustain the practice of innovation-led growth by broadening sources of revenue from multiple innovations within the functional activities of the organization. Therefore, the purpose of the innovation impact criterion is to examine the extent to which the goal is being achieved.

• That, innovation impact criterion has been applied to all the revenue generated by the organization's core functional units and to the cost savings gained from support functional units.

• That, the innovation impact criterion has been applied to both radical and incremental innovations launched or implemented during the period under review.

- You could also include a note that details of the innovation impact criterion are interpreted in the innovation performance data and evaluative questions section of the report.

5. Innovation Performance Data and Evaluative Questions

In the preceding section (i.e. evaluation criteria), we have described how each evaluation criterion should be presented when writing the evaluation report.

As seen from the subtitle, this section is separated in two parts: *Innovation Performance Data* (Part I) and *Evaluative Questions* (Part II). We begin the discussion with:

Part I: Innovation Performance Data

The purpose of this section is to outline innovation performance data as being a result of the various innovation-support programs implemented during the period under review. This is vital because it is on this data that the evaluation of the HR innovation-support strategy will be based. With that in mind, it is important to use simple presentation formats and styles that are easy to understand by workforces.

Here are some examples of aspects that would be included in this section:

- Outline the importance of the data that is being presented in determining the final assessment of whether the HR innovation-support strategy under review is successful.

- That, the information generated from data presented is useful for determining the innovation-performance status of the organization in terms of whether the innovation goals, objectives, and targets that were set by various functional units have been achieved.

- That, the innovation performance data presented is interpreted in the context of each of the four evaluation criteria listed below for the evaluation of the HR innovation-support strategy under review. As mentioned, the four evaluation criteria are:

  ○ Relevance and efficiency of the innovation inputs
  ○ Innovation ideation
  ○ Innovation results
  ○ Innovation impact

Illustration

In this section, we provide examples of how to relate the innovation performance data presented earlier (in Tables 5-9 to 5-22) to each of the four evaluation criteria listed above.

Relevance and Efficiency of Innovation-Inputs Criterion

Based on the definition of the relevance and efficiency of innovation-inputs criterion provided earlier, this section should do two things: (1)outline the innovation-support programs implemented during the period under review and (2) interpret the context of the relevancy and efficiency of innovation-input criterion in relation to examining the success of the innovation support programs implemented during the period under review.

As an example, Tables 5-26, 5-27 and 5-28 illustrate how to relate the relevance and efficiency of innovation-inputs criterion to innovation-support programs implemented during the period under review.

Table 5-26. Relevance and efficiency of the innovation inputs (*innovation management programs*)

HR innovation-support strategy Evaluation criteria February – December, 2020		
Category A: Innovation management programs		
Innovation-support programs implemented	Relevance	Efficiency
• Identifying and creating innovation priority areas (IPAs) • Interpreting and creating dimensions of innovation • Translating the meaning of innovation in the context of • Formulating organizational innovation goals • Creating innovation roles • Creating innovation-challenge questions • Innovation-idea management system	Each of the programs was created, tailored, and implemented based on priority and need consistent with purpose and goals of the HR innovation-support strategy under review	• 9 out of 11 programs are up and running • 5 booklets covering all the 9 innovation practices have been created and circulated to all the workforces as planned • 20 training sessions (virtual and in-person) on various topics of innovation were conducted as planned • 3 programs have overlapped their implementation timeframe

• Creating a mechanism for identifying and hiring innovation talent		
• Creating a framework for innovation talent succession planning		
• Creating a framework for measuring and reporting innovation performance		

Table 5-27. Relevance and efficiency of the innovation inputs (*innovative thinking programs*)

HR innovation-support strategy Evaluation criteria February – December, 2020		
Category B: **Innovative thinking programs**		
Innovation-support programs implemented	**Relevance**	**Efficiency**
• Questioning attribute • Associating attribute • Experimenting attribute • Networking attribute	Each of the programs was created, tailored and implemented based on priority and need consistent with purpose and goals of the HR innovation-support strategy under review	• A booklet covering all the 11 attributes of innovative thinking was created and accessed by all the workforces as planned

• Envisioning attribute • No fear-of-failure attribute • Risk-taking attribute • Challenging-status-quo attribute • Grit attribute • Thinking time attribute • Role-modeling in leading a culture of innovation		• A total of 15 training sessions (virtual and in-person) on all the 11innovative thinking attributes were conducted as planned

Table 5-28. Relevance and efficiency of the innovation inputs (*innovation engagement programs*)

HR innovation-support strategy Evaluation criteria February – December, 2020		
Category C: **Innovation engagement programs** *(Using informative and inspirational styles)*		
Informative	**Relevance**	**Efficiency**

style: Educate workforces about the company's innovation strategies, practices and policies implemented during the period under review	Each program and activity were created, tailored, and implemented based on priority and need consistent with purpose and goals of the HR innovation-support strategy under review	• Introduced an innovation newsletter aimed at informing workforces about the company's:
		
		  ○ Innovation strategies, policies, and procedures
		
		  ○ Innovation ideas generated
		
		  ○ Innovations launched or implemented

		o New markets
		o Revenues generated by various innovations
		o Cost saving gained from innovations
		• Video and audio recording of the CEO's statements on the company's innovation efforts and achievement
		• Introduced monthly "innovation town hall" meetings to be addressed by the CEO
		• Introduced departmental meetings on innovation addressed by heads of departments and other senior managers
		• Established an "Annual Innovation Day" conducted second Friday of August
		• Created innovation-related phrases inscribed on various company themed items i.e. mugs, T-shirts, bags, pens, diaries water bottles etc.
		All the activities were implemented as planned
Inspirational style: Created innovation-motivating slogans, catchphrases, and visual	**Relevance**	**Efficiency**
	Each program and activity were created, tailored, and implemented based on priority and need consistent	• 20 innovation-motivating slogans posted around the company • 15 innovation-motivating catchphrases posted around the company

illustrations for instilling innovation in the hearts and minds of workforces	with purpose and goals of the HR innovation-support strategy under review	• 10 innovation-motivating visual illustrations posted around the company All the activities were implemented as planned

Innovation Ideation Criterion

The innovation ideation criterion entails the overall number of innovation ideas generated across the company as a consequence of the implementation of the HR innovation-support strategy. So, this section should provide data relating to the number of radical and incremental innovation ideas generated during the period under review. And remember, this is the data on which the evaluative question will be based, as well as the overall conclusion of the evaluation report.

Earlier in this chapter in Step Two (on measuring innovation performance), we used tables to show innovation ideas generated and those undergoing development. We've used the same data to show, by use of simple charts the number of radical and incremental innovation ideas generated in both the core and support functional units of Walu Technologies for the period under review.

For purposes of this illustration, Figure 5-1 shows the combined number of radical and incremental innovation ideas generated by all the three product segments of Walu Technologies product development division (software, cloud storage and cybersecurity).

Figure 5- 1. Radical and incremental innovation ideas generated

Number of radical and incremental product innovation ideas
generated
February - December, 2020

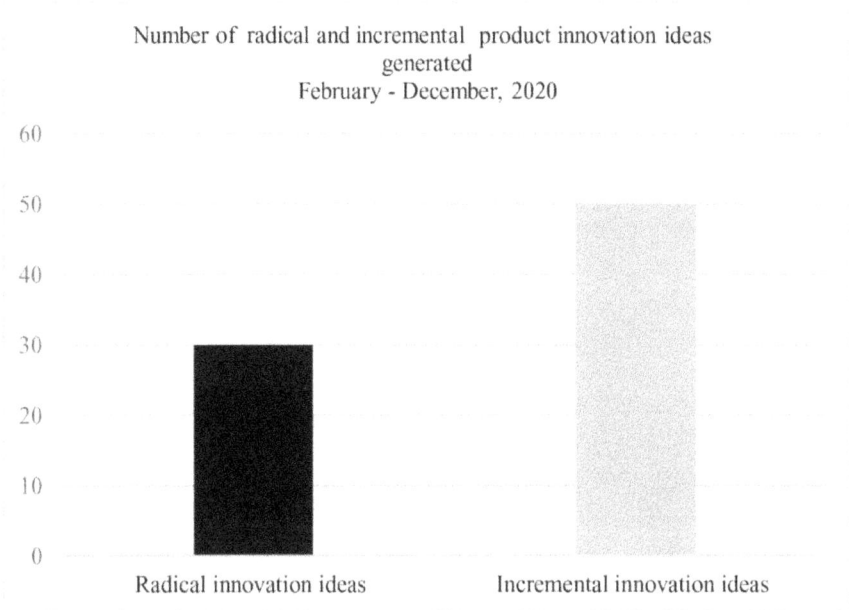

Similar charts will be created for innovation ideas generated in the other core and support functional units covered earlier in Step Two (Marketing and customer service departments, procurement, HR, finance and accounting, and IT departments).

Innovation Results Criterion

The same approach used in the preceding section on innovation ideation is applied here. So, this criterion presents data on the number of innovations launched or implemented during the period under review. This is the data on which the evaluative question will be based, and the overall conclusion written into the evaluation report.

For illustration purposes, the chart below (Figure 5-2) shows the combined number of radical and incremental innovations launched by the three product segments of Walu Technologies product development division (software, cloud storage, and cybersecurity). Data used for this chart is adopted from table 5-14 in Step Two on measuring innovation performance which we discussed earlier.

Figure 5-2. Number of radical and incremental innovations launched

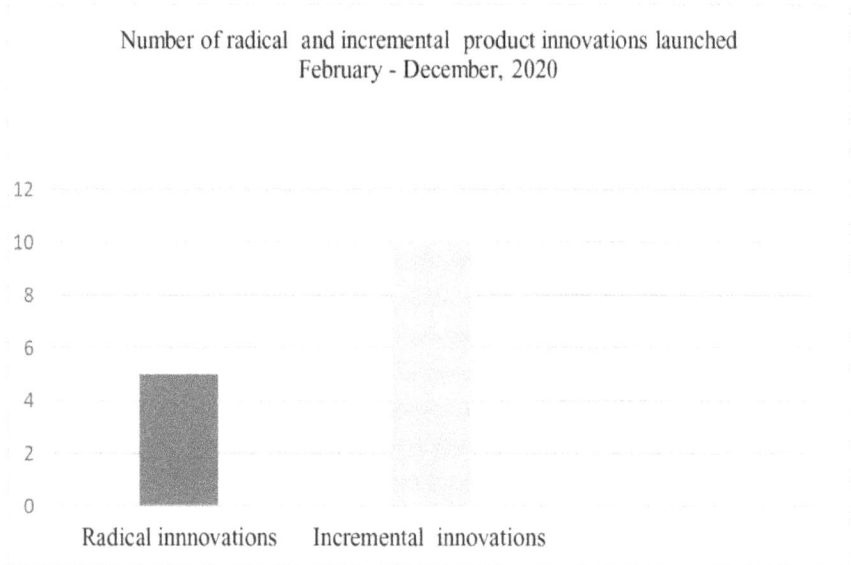

Number of radical and incremental product innovations launched
February - December, 2020

Similar charts would be created for innovations launched or implemented in the other core and support functional units covered earlier in Step Two, i.e. Marketing and Customer Service Departments. And support functional units, procurement, HR, finance and accounting, and IT departments.

Innovation Impact Criterion

The innovation impact criterion provides data that informs whether the monetary goals of the innovation-support strategy were achieved. In this section, you would show two data points: (1) revenue generated by innovations launched and (2) cost savings gained from innovation implemented during the period under review. Again, this is the data on which the evaluative question will be based and the overall conclusion of the evaluation report.

Figure 5-3 shown below illustrates the combined revenue generated by radical and incremental innovations launched by the three product categories of Walu Technologies product development division (software, cloud storage and cybersecurity solutions).

Figure 5-3. Revenue generated

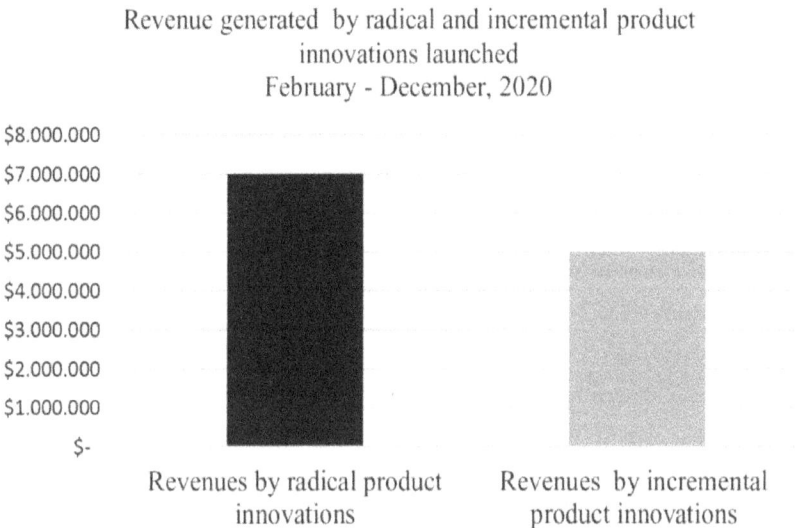

Revenue generated by radical and incremental product
innovations launched
February - December, 2020

$8.000.000	
$7.000.000	
$6.000.000	
$5.000.000	
$4.000.000	
$3.000.000	
$2.000.000	
$1.000.000	
$-	
Revenues by radical product innovations	Revenues by incremental product innovations

Again, similar charts would be created for other core and support functional units covered earlier in Step Two. And support functional units, procurement, HR, finance and accounting, and IT departments.

Part II Evaluative Questions

Remember, we have two parts in number five of this section (Part I: Innovation performance data and Part II: Evaluative questions).

This section looks at *evaluative questions*. The purpose of the evaluative questions is twofold: (1) to ask questions that relate to the data presented in Part I and (2) use the answers elicited from the evaluative questions to draw inferences and conclusions. The conclusions are on two aspects: (1) whether the HR innovation-support strategy under review would be deemed a success and (2) an explanation either way (the reasons for success—or if no success, why).

So, when writing the evaluation report, this section should have an evaluative-questions worksheet or table with questions that reflect the evaluation criteria factors presented earlier (in Part I—on *innovation performance data*). There are many styles or formats for presenting evaluative questions. As an example, we have used four tables to illustrate evaluative questions for assessing each of the four evaluation criteria stated in Tables 5-29, 5-30, 5-31, and 5-32.

Table 5-29. Example of evaluative question worksheet for assessing *relevancy and efficiency of innovation-inputs criterion*

Evaluative question worksheet
Category of innovation-support program: *Innovation management*
Date: December 28, 2020
Time frame under review: February – December, 2020
Objective: *To determine whether innovation management-related programs implemented during the period under review (February– December of 2020) met or exceeded the relevancy and efficiency of innovation-inputs criterion.*
Evaluative question Based on the relevancy and efficiency of innovation inputs criterion data presented earlier (in Part I, *innovation performance data*), state whether innovation management-related programs implemented during the period under review *met or exceeded* the relevancy and efficiency of innovation-inputs criterion.
Innovation management programs implemented

Did the innovation management program listed below **meet or exceed** the relevancy and efficiency of innovation-inputs criterion? (check "Yes" or "No")	Yes	Comment	No	Comment
		Reasons: If yes, *what factors would be responsible for meeting or exceeding the set criterion?*		Reasons: *If no, what factors would be responsible for not meeting the set criterion?*
Innovation priority areas (IPAs)				
Interpreting and creating dimensions of innovation				
Translating the meaning of innovation				
Formulating organizational innovation goals				
Creating innovation roles				
Creating innovation-challenge questions				
Innovation-idea management system				
Identifying and hiring innovation talent				

Measuring and reporting innovation performance				

Similar evaluative question worksheets would be created for the other two categories of innovation-support programs:

- Innovative thinking programs
- Innovation engagement programs

Table 5-30. Example of an evaluative question worksheet for assessing *innovation ideation criterion*

Name of department: Product development division				
Product segments being assessed: Software, cloud storage, and cybersecurity				
Date: December 28, 2020				
Innovation ideation: *To assess whether the number of radical and incremental product innovation ideas generated in all the three product segments of Walu Technologies met or exceeded the goal during the period under review (February –December of 2020).*				
Evaluative question **Whether the number of radical and incremental product innovation ideas generated *met or exceeded* the goal**				
Radical innovations launched				
Radical	**Yes**	**Comment**	**No**	**Comment**
innovation ideas innovation ideas generated in the product-development division: *Was the goal achieved?* (check "**Yes**" or "**No**")		If yes, indicate the percentage achieved. **Reasons:** *What factors would be responsible for meeting or exceeding the set goal?*		If no, by what percentage was the goal missed? **Reasons:** *What factors would be responsible for not meeting the projected goal?*
Incremental innovation ideas generated				

Incremental innovation ideas innovation ideas generated in the product-development division: *Was the goal achieved?* (check "**Yes**" or "**No**")	Yes	Comment	No	Comment
		If yes, indicate the percentage achieved. **Reasons:** *What factors would be responsible for meeting or exceeding the set goal?*		If no, by what percentage was the goal missed? **Reasons:** *What factors would be responsible for not meeting the projected goal?*

Table 5-31. Example of evaluative question worksheet for assessing *innovation results criterion*

Name of department: Product-development division
Product segments being assessed: Software, cloud storage, and cybersecurity
Date: December 28, 2020
Innovation results: *To assess whether the number of radical and incremental product innovations launched in all three product segments of Walu Technologies met or exceeded the goal during the period under review (February –December of 2020).*
Evaluative question   **Whether the number of radical and incremental product innovations launched *met or exceeded* the goal**
Radical innovations launched

Radical innovation ideas innovations launched in the product-development division: *Was the goal achieved?* (check "**Yes**" or "**No**")	Yes	Comment	No	Comment
		If yes, indicate the percentage achieved. Reasons: What factors could be responsible for meeting or exceeding the set goal?		If no, by what percentage was the goal missed? Reasons: What factors could be responsible for not meeting the projected goal?

Incremental innovation ideas generated

Incremental innovation ideas innovation launched in the product-development division: *Was the goal achieved?* (check **"Yes"** or **"No"**)	Yes	Comment	No	Comment
		If yes, indicate the percentage achieved. **Reasons:** *What factors are responsible for meeting or exceeding the set goal?*		If no, by what percentage was the goal missed? **Reasons:** *What factors are responsible for not meeting the projected goal?*

Table 5-32. Example of evaluative question worksheet for assessing *innovation impact criterion*

Name of Department: Product development division
Product segments being assessed: Software, cloud storage, and cybersecurity
Date: December 28, 2020
Innovation impact: *To assess whether the goal of generating a particular amount of revenue from various radical and incremental product innovations launched during the period under review (February –December of 2020), was achieved.*
Evaluative question **Whether the revenue generated by radical and incremental product innovations launched during the period under review *met or exceeded* the goal**
Radical innovations: **Revenue generated from radical innovations launched during the period under review**

Was the goal achieved? (check **"Yes"** or **"No"**)	Yes	Comment	No	Comment
		If yes, indicate the percentage achieved. **Reasons:** *What factors are responsible for achieving or exceeding the set goal?*		If no, by what percentage was the goal missed? **Reasons:** *What factors are responsible for not meeting the projected goal?*

Incremental innovations: **Revenue generated from radical innovations launched during the period under review**				
Was the	**Yes**	**Comment**	**No**	**Comment**
goal achieved? (check **"Yes"** or **"No"**)		If yes, indicate the percentage achieved. **Reasons:** *What factors are responsible for meeting or exceeding the set goal?*		If no, by what percentage was the goal missed? **Reasons:** *What factors are responsible for not meeting the projected goal?*

Innovation-Life Time Frame

One of the aspects to include at the end of the evaluation report is a statement on the innovation-life time frame. What does *innovation-life time frame* mean? It is a period set by an organization within which an innovation will qualify to be called or characterized as an innovation and after which it will cease to be called or characterized as such.

The innovation-life time frame is vital when it comes to assessing and reporting the impact on monetary value because only innovations that have not elapsed should be included in subsequent innovation-performance reports.

Therefore, one of the initial tasks to undertake when adopting a framework for innovation-performance reporting is to define the period within which an innovation will carry the *innovation* tag. This would be done by stating the expiration time frame in terms of when an innovation will cease to be referred to as an innovation in the evaluation report. Once the period elapses, the innovation—whether a product innovation, process innovation, marketing innovation, etc.—will no longer carry the innovation tag and will be referred to using the same terminology as that used for other existing product offerings, process components, marketing components, customer service components or support functional units.

Is there a standard time period for an innovation-life time frame? The time frame varies from company to company, depending on the innovation-performance framework of the organization. Thus, the company must clearly define the innovation-life time period, which should be communicated to all the workforces across functional units. For instance, "Any type and degree of innovation shall be referred to as an innovation for no more than three years. After three years, such a product, process, marketing component, or any other type of innovation shall no longer carry the innovation tag or be referred to as an innovation."

6. Conclusion and Improvements

Are we finally finished with the evaluation process? Yes, we're done! The conclusion is the final part of the journey, i.e. the HR innovation-support strategy implementation process.

Remember, the purpose of initiating an HR innovation-support strategy is twofold: (1) to help functional units achieve their innovation performance goals, and (2) to help the organization to make innovation a habitual and permanent practice across all functional units (i.e. build a culture of innovation). As stated earlier, the sole purpose of the evaluation process is to examine and find out if the HR innovation-support strategy implementation process lived to its expectation.

Since this section provides the answer to whether HR innovation-support strategy implementation process lived to its expectation, avoid the temptation of "data rich but information poor" (DRIP) situations. So, this section should summarize the information in the two preceding sections (I.e. innovation performance data and evaluative questions). We provide examples as follows:

Table 5-33 provides summaries of conclusions based on the evaluation criteria and information elicited from the innovation performance data and evaluative questions.

Table 5-33. Summaries of conclusion

Summaries of conclusion for innovation-support programs implemented February-December, 2020		
Innovation management programs	**Innovative thinking programs**	**Innovation engagement programs**
Comments: Implementation of the prioritized programs in this category was a success. For	*Comments:* Implementation of programs in this category was a success. All the	*Comments:* All programs in this category were implemented successfully. For
example, 81 percent of the programs are up and running within the timeframe. Only 9 percent of the programs were not implemented. All 20 training sessions were conducted and only 3 programs overlapped their implementation timeframe.	programs were based on priority. A booklet covering the 11 attributes of innovative thinking was created and distributed to all workforces. And a total of 15 training sessions on all the 11innovative thinking attributes were conducted as planned.	instance, an innovation newsletter, video, and audio recording of the CEO, innovation departmental meetings, annual innovation day have been introduced during the period under review.
Summaries of conclusion for February – December 2020		
Innovation performance during the period under review was a success based on the three perspectives stated below.		
Innovation ideas generated	**Innovations launched/ implemented**	**Monetary gained**

175

Both radical and incremental innovation ideas generated exceeded the set goal. There was a combined total of 80 innovation ideas generated across all functional units.	Both radical and incremental innovations launched or implemented exceeded the set goals. There was a combined total of 15 innovations launched and implemented across all functional units.	The revenues generated by both radical and incremental innovations launched and cost savings gained from radical and incremental innovations implemented exceeded the set goals. About $12,000,000 was contributed in terms of revenue generated and cost savings gained.

Weaknesses and improvements

This section should highlight some weaknesses and improvements to the process of developing and implementing the HR innovation-support strategy. For instance, you could, identify weaknesses at specific phases of the HR innovation-support strategy i.e. weaknesses at the analysis phase, or priority and implementation phases. Example of the weaknesses could include:

- An overload of innovation-support programs identified/ prioritized for implementation.

- Weak collaboration with other functional units during implementation and evaluation phases of the HR innovation-support strategy

- No survey conducted to gather opinion from workforces across functional units about the HR innovation-support strategy process and outcome.

Examples of suggestions and improvements could be based on the identified weaknesses. The improvements should be considered in the next year or cycle of the HR innovation-support strategy.

SUMMARY

Let's recap the six main aspects this book has covered.

1. Since innovation is a process that involves unlocking human capital to generate innovative ideas, HR is best suited for driving workforce innovation.

2. Study after study reveals that the challenge faced by many HR professionals is how to continually create and implement innovation-support strategies and programs that contribute to institutionalizing workforce innovation in the organization.

3. HR professionals cannot meaningfully contribute to advancing innovation or creating a culture of innovation using traditional HR tools and practices.

4. HR innovation-support strategy is a step-by-step process expressed in detailed statements of how various innovation-related tools, approaches, and actions can be applied by HR to implement initiatives aimed at advancing workforce innovation across functional units to achieve a culture of innovation.

5. The HR innovation-support strategy models as framework for designing and implementing innovation-related programs and actions to make innovation a habitual practice across the organization; and it helps the organization achieve innovation goals.

6. The HR innovation-support strategy adopted in this book is structured in four phases:

- Preliminary steps to undertake
- Analysis
- Implementation
- Evaluation

SELECTED REFERENCES

Brian Becker, The *HR Scorecard: Linking People, Strategy, and Performance*,

Harvard Business Review Press,2001

Dave Ulrich, *HR from the Outside In: Six Competencies for the Future of Human Resources*, McGraw-Hill Education, 2012

David Masumba, *Leadership for Innovation*, New York, Morgan James Publishing, 2019

David Masumba, *Innovation Talent Succession Planning,* KDP, 2020

David Masumba, *How to Measure and Report Innovation Performance,* KDP, 2020

David Masumba, *How to Evaluate Innovation Performance of Workforces*, KDP, 2020

David Masumba, Hiring for Innovation, KDP, 2020

Gerry Johnson, et al*, Exploring Corporate Strategy*, 8th Edition, Prentice Hall, 2008

Rowan Gibson*, Innovation to the Core: A Blueprint for Transforming the Way Your Company Innovates*, Harvard Business Review Press, 2008

Economist Intelligence: http://www.oracle.com/us/products/applications/eiu-oracle-bus-innovation-1867915.pdf

Harvard Business Review Publishing : https://hbr.org/2008/05/innovation-advice-from-procter

Accenture: https://www.marketwatch.com/press-release/
accenture-study-innovation-efforts-falling-short-despite-increased-
investment-2013-05-13

The Conference Board CEO Challenge 2015 Research
Report: https://www.conference-board.org/retrievefile.
cfm?filename=TCB_1570_15_RR_CEO_Challenge3.
pdf&type=subsite

https://www.pwc.com/gx/en/ceo-survey/2017/deep-dives/ceo-survey-
global-talent.pdf?fbclid=IwAR0WhcJ9dw15bMXd7QSl6f2tsIhOSK
8looaK_-G5YzvKeTXLL9Ite8hDPfY

https://conference-board.org/topics/future-of-innovation